Servant Leadership

A Better Way to do Business

Dustin Danny Hofheins, MBA

About the Author

Dustin Danny Hofheins holds two master's degrees in business administration. He is a Job Coach for a non-profit organization and has been a student of servant leadership for over ten years.

Abstract

Servant leadership is a practical leadership method that focuses on the leader serving the needs of the employees, customers, and the organization. The leadership roles of the organization are a stewardship, resulting in the manager/executive serving all the critical aspects of the organization in an effective way. The servant leader places a large emphasis on serving and developing the greatest asset of the organization, which is the employees. Serving and developing the needs of employees benefits the organization by way of reduced turnover rates, increased employee loyalty, increased employee satisfaction, increased employee productivity, and reduced training costs. *Servant Leadership: A Better Way to do Business*, contains the research and findings from a servant leadership study that Dustin conducted, and has the potential to revolutionize the way you approach business and leadership.

There is a gap in the research regarding the role of love in servant leadership. This study explores the relationship and importance of love within the construct of servant leadership theory. For the purposes of this research, love was not defined as a feeling;

love is defined as an action verb. Love is defined as the leader's ability to serve his or her constituents. The researcher utilized a qualitative research method, which drew on real-life experiences from self-declared servant leaders. The researcher employed ten semi-structured open-ended interviews to gather the data. The researcher utilized NVivo qualitative data analysis software to find key themes from the interview data. After thematic analysis of the interview data, key themes were discovered. The themes found for the role of love in servant leadership are the following: people, caring, serve, feeling, and relationships. The themes found for the significance of love in today's leadership culture are the following: people, feeling, different, better, and world.

Keywords: servant leadership, servant leader, leadership, service, love, agape love

Dedication

I would like to dedicate this book to my wonderful wife, Zoe Hofheins, and our amazing children; Kayleigh, Mason, Crew, and Sadie Hofheins. All have sacrificed much for me to work toward my outlandish goals.

Acknowledgments

I would like to thank my wonderful wife, Zoe Hofheins, for being the kind of wife that continually encouraged and supported my educational endeavors. I would like to thank my mother-in-law Linda Arrowsmith for helping our family in times of need along this journey. I would like to thank my father, Dan Hofheins, for not allowing me to become a partner in the family masonry business and telling me that I needed to go back to college so that I could provide a better life for my family. I would like to thank my father-in-law Stephen Arrowsmith, MA, for taking me under his wing regarding the completion of this book. I would also like to thank my mother, Kaye Hofheins, for her unwavering encouragement, sacrifice, and financial support.

Table of Contents

Chapter 1

Introduction to Study

Robert K. Greenleaf (1977) asserted that there was a leadership crisis in America. and I would argue that there still is a leadership crisis 42 years later. A 2015 Gallup Poll surveyed over 7,200 individuals and found that over half of all surveyed had previously left a job to get away from a "bad manager" (Harter & Adkins, 2015). I contend that it is the leadership style of the "bad managers" that contributes to over half of the American workforce quitting. Servant leadership is a leadership theory that places an emphasis on the leader serving the needs of all the stakeholders of the organization, placing a high priority on meeting the needs of employees. This style of leadership has been proven to increase employee satisfaction and decrease employee turnover (Jichul & Kandampully, 2017; McCann, Graves, & Cox, 2014). In a current literature review of servant leadership, it was found that there is a gap in the research regarding the role of love in servant leadership theory. Love is often a topic that is not associated with leadership, because of leaderships historically masculine nature. The researcher has chosen to follow the recommendations of many current researchers to explore the role of love in servant leadership (Harper, 2017; Sullivan, 2017; Nishii, 2017; Rajek, 2014; Ricciardi, 2014).

Background of the Study

The leadership style of servant leadership has roots that stretch back to ancient times. For example, Jesus Christ stated: "But he that is greatest among you shall be your servant" (Matt. 23:11, King James Version). Zentner (2015), in a study that compared the values of the major religions of the world to the values of servant leadership, found the following religions to have rooted values that are in harmony with servant leadership: Buddhism, Christianity, Confucianism, Hinduism, Islam, Jainism, Judaism, Shinto, Sikhism, Taoism, and Zoroastrianism. Greenleaf (1977) brought servant leadership as a leadership model into focus in the 1970s, and interest and academic research regarding the topic of servant leadership has slowly increased since. Greenleaf stated that servant leaders first must have a natural desire to serve others, then aspire to lead. Greenleaf also asserted that servant leaders serve the needs of the employees and customers to create a more caring and just society. Research regarding love and servant leadership is a concept that has not been thoroughly explored, and as a result there is little academic research that combines the two concepts. This research seeks to combine the concepts of love and servant leadership in an exploratory research format.

Problem Statement

The researcher completed a qualitative study, which examined the lived experiences of participants. The study examined the role of love in the leadership theory of servant leadership. Focht and Ponton (2015) reported that 86% percent of participants agreed, or strongly agreed, that love is a primary characteristic of servant leadership. Harper (2017) recommended that future research should focus on love and leadership. Sullivan recommended future research regarding love, forgiveness, and leadership (Sullivan, 2017). Rajek suggested that future research needs to be conducted to determine how love can be increased, and that this research should then be infused into servant leadership development (Rajek, 2014). Ricciardi suggested future research identifying love and leadership effectiveness because of the links between love and leadership (Ricciardi, 2014). Nishii recommended a qualitative study with the topic including love and servant leadership (Nishii, 2017). The preceding researchers studied various aspects of love and/or leadership, however each researcher recommended that future research needs to be done regarding the topic of love and leadership. The problem is a lack of research regarding the role of love in servant leadership.

Purpose Statement

The purpose of this study was to examine the role of love in servant leadership through the lived experiences of participants. The researcher explored the extent to which love plays a part in the servant leadership framework. A deeper understanding of the definition of love, as it relates to servant leadership, provided valuable knowledge and added to the limited body of research.

Research Questions

RQ1 What is the role of love in servant leadership?

RQ2 What do you think is the significance of love in today's leadership culture?

Advancing Theoretical Knowledge

Servant leadership theory forms the theoretical framework for this paper. The father of servant leadership theory is Robert K. Greenleaf with his 1977 article titled *Servant Leadership: A Journey into the Nature of Legitimate Power and Greatness*. Greenleaf asserted that a leader should serve his or her employees and serve them first. Greenleaf also suggested that servant leaders first seek to serve others, and then aspire to lead. Focht and Ponton (2015) identified the twelve characteristics of servant leaders: valuing people, humble, listening, trusting, caring, having integrity, serving, empowering, serving others' needs before their own, collaborating, loving unconditionally, and learning.

Love is one of many characteristics that have been identified in servant leadership theory. Greenleaf (1977) stated: "Love without laughter can be grim and oppressive. Laughter without love can be divisive and venomous. Together they make for greatness of spirit." Aristotle stated: "Happiness is the meaning and the purpose of life, the whole aim and end of human existence. Wicked men obey from fear; good men, from love" (Aristotle, trans. 1931). Love for the purposes of this research will be defined not as romantic love but as an agape love that motivates the servant leader to serve the needs of his or her employees and customers.

While romantic love does happen in the workplace, romantic love is not a characteristic within the servant leadership list of characteristics. Love means the leader is being accountable for the development and success of employees. Love is treating employees in the way that you would want to be treated. Love is creating a work environment that is a little more enjoyable to work in. Love is caring enough about an employee to encourage and lift him or her to greatness. Focht and Ponton (2015) asserted that if you start from the standpoint of unconditional love—meaning that you believe every individual is valuable, and you also believe in being committed to treat every individual and circumstance with the most love possible—it transforms the way that you treat others, and you have a clearer understanding of your higher purpose. When you approach difficult business situations with love, the difficult situations are resolved in a way that keeps the morale and productivity of the employees up.

The leader who can show love to his or her employees through selfless service is better able to make a lasting impact on the employee, thus increasing the value of the employee to the organization. This phenomenon of employee development through the action of love is of critical importance because employees have other options available to them for employment.

The researcher argues that developing employees to become the best employees available adds value to the organization and reduces employee turnover. The personal experiences of the participants add depth and perspective to a complex subject. Although personal experiences are difficult to quantify, it does not make the experiences any less valuable in research. The concept of showing love to employees through the construct of servant leadership theory is so new that this research added critical and valuable knowledge to servant leadership practice.

Significance of the Study

The findings of this study added to the love and servant leadership body of knowledge and research. Business administration practitioners, and all leaders alike can apply the results of this study to current business and leadership practices. The findings, if applied to practice, have the potential of increasing organizational health, increasing organizational performance, increasing employee retention rates, increasing employee productivity, increasing employee satisfaction, increasing referent power, increasing customer loyalty, etc.

Nishii (2017) stated –

Servant leaders dare to walk on the narrow ridge without clear answers or recipes to follow whether it is related to love, relationships, or power (or a combination of them). Further understanding of such experience through the phenomenological and hermeneutic approach would add value not only to the scholarly knowledge, but also to the practitioners of servant leadership.

Definition of Terms

Agape love. The highest form of love, godlike love and charity. Loving others without expectations for anything in return.

Love. An action verb meaning that if we truly love others, we serve them.

Servant leadership. A theory in which the leader is a servant first, and then aspires to lead. The servant leader serves his or her employees' and customers' first.

Assumptions, Limitations, and Delimitations

This section covers assumptions, limitations, and delimitations found in this research.

Assumptions

The researcher provided definitions for both servant leadership and love as defined by the study to participants to provide a common basis for participants to answer interview questions. It is assumed that participants will answer the questions truthfully. If participants do not answer the questions truthfully, then the accuracy of the study would be negatively affected. The researcher also assumed that the participants who agreed to participate in the study wanted to do so. Not wanting to participate in the study, and still doing so, could lead the participant to hurriedly go through the study, and not take the time to understand and answer each question thoroughly.

Limitations

There are many limitations to this study. One such limitation is that the results of the study cannot be generalized to include servant leaders in all organizations, because of the limited numeral quantity of participants, and the limited geographical area of the study. However, one could take the results of this study and compare it with future studies from other geographical locations. Another limitation of this study is that the participants have personal biases, such as personal preferences toward a certain leadership style, that, in turn, may affect the results of the study. Participants may not take the time to honestly answer the questions, which could also limit the accuracy of the study results, as mentioned earlier. There may be other research tools that could study the role of love in servant leadership in a more accurate way.

Delimitations

The researcher limited the geographical area of the study to self-declared servant leaders located in Salt Lake County, Utah County, Wasatch County, Iron County, Washington County and Summit County, within the State of Utah, and in the United States of America. This limitation is due to the limited resources available to the researcher. Because of this limitation, the results of the study cannot be generalized. The researcher limited the study to self-declared servant leaders of organizations who have leadership experience for over five years. The researcher limited the study to only paid leaders of the organizations. Volunteers or members of advisory boards were excluded from the study. The definition of love was limited to the leader's ability to show love through serving his or her employees. Love that is defined by romanticism is not applicable to servant leadership theory and will therefore be excluded from the study and literature review.

Summary and Organization of the Remainder of the Study

In order to bring all the concepts into alignment, the following literature review includes the historical study of love, such as agape love. The literature review also presents a historical study of servant leadership, leading up to the relevance of servant leadership theory.

Chapter 2

Literature Review

The theory of servant leadership applies directly to business administration because it is a leadership model that can be utilized by the business leaders of the 21st century. Hodoh (2016) found that the employees of servant leaders have a higher productivity rate than leaders who are not servant leaders. Coetzer, Bussin, and Geldenhuys (2017) found that employees of servant leaders have a lower work burnout rate when compared to other leadership styles. Jichul, Kandampully, McCann, Graves, and Cox (2017) found that servant leadership has been proven to increase employee satisfaction and decrease employee turnover. Coetzer, Bussin, and Geldenhuys found in comparative literature review of servant leadership that it has a positive correlation with employee performance and employee organizational commitment (Coetzer, Bussin, & Geldenhuys, 2017). Preiksaitis stated that business researchers have found that servant leaders empower, provide long-term vision, and serve the needs of employees in a more effective way than other styles of leadership

(Preiksaitis, 2016). Hargadon (2018) argued that servant leadership can be utilized by business leaders to create a business environment where stress is reduced, and employees are happier. Servant leadership goes against the command-and-control style of leadership that many business leaders have utilized in the past and will likely continue to use in the future (Ebener & O'Connell, 2010). Servant leaders are motivated by love and stewardship, while command and control leaders are motivated to achieve results through micromanagement, fear, power, and selfishness. This study of the role of love in servant leadership, as applied to business administration, is critical to the future success of business researchers, and practitioners.

The topic of love applies directly to business administration because love is such an essential component within the servant leadership model (Focht & Ponton, 2015). Ricciardi found that leaders who demonstrate a love for their employees are perceived by followers as being more effective leaders than leaders who do not demonstrate love to employees (Ricciardi, 2014). Sullivan stated that love and forgiveness are critical components of an effective leadership style (Sullivan, 2017). Love can be viewed as a negative by some leaders who view leadership from a position of command and control.

Love within the servant leadership model allows for business leaders to fill the needs of employees, customers, and the organization through being an effective steward over each area. Love encourages servant leaders to serve the needs of not just the employees, but all the stakeholders of the business. Love encourages a culture of employee development in which business leaders facilitate the upward movement and forward momentum of the employees of the organization. The researcher argues that business leaders and entrepreneurs of the 21st century would benefit the organizations they represent by creating a servant leadership culture that is centered on love, because employee loyalty, and employee productivity would increase. Love directly applies to business administration because when business leaders lead with love the organization will be led ethically, efficiently, and with an effective stewardship.

This study is critical to the study and practice of business administration because servant leadership is a theory that is often misunderstood or unheard of by business practitioners (Sullivan,

2017). However, servant leadership is a theory that if applied to the culture of an organization can result in happier employees, happier customers, and increased financial performance. This study increases the awareness of servant leadership theory to business leaders and will add an increased understanding of the theory of servant leadership by exploring the role that love plays within the theory.

Love

The literature review of love will help provide a theoretical lens for which to understand how the term *love* will be viewed in this research. For the purpose of this study and literature review, love was not defined as romantic love, or feelings that come as a result of romanticism. Love is defined as the leader's ability to serve the needs of his or her employees. Agape love is a definition of love that can be applied to servant leadership. Agape love is godlike love for an individual. Agape love is charity. Agape love is having the best interest of others as the leader's primary motivator. Robinson stated: "What characterizes this kind of love is that it's not primarily a love of the emotions. Agape love is a mindset, an orientation of the will. Agape love determines that it will seek the highest good for other people" (Robinson, 2015). Robinson argued that agape love is not so much a feeling, but a state of mind. He asserted that an individual could decide that he or she will not harm another, not respond cursing for cursing, or vile for vile (Robinson, 2015). Lewis stated that agape flows from the heart and not from the loins (Lewis, 1963). Gonwa asserted that agape love increases in an individual as the individual draws closer to God (Gonwa, 2015)

Kauffman argued that dedicating one's life to agape results in brotherly and sisterly love (Kauffman, 2013). Goodier and Eisenberg found in an ethnographic study that 84 percent of study participants considered spirituality to be demonstrated as love (Goodier & Eisenberg, 2006). Halter asserted that great leaders see the importance of leading from a foundation of love (Halter, 2006). Ricciardi found that leaders who demonstrate love in their leadership abilities are perceived as having a higher level of leadership when compared to a leader who does not demonstrate love in their leadership style (Ricciardi, 2014). Ginoza declared that it is love that serves as the healer of broken relationships, and of societies (Ginoza, 1976). Bekker argued that love is the source of personal power

(Bekker, 2009). A passage in Corinthians in the Bible states how important love is:

> Though I speak with the tongues of men and of angels, but have not love, I have become sounding brass or a clanging cymbal. And though I have the gift of prophecy, and understand all mysteries and all knowledge, and though I have all faith, so that I could remove mountains, but have not love, I am nothing. And though I bestow all my goods to feed the poor, and though I give my body to be burned, but have not love, it profits me nothing. (1 Cor. 13:1–4, The New King James Version).

Corinthians also supplies a definition of love that provides the framework for the following literature review regarding love.

> Love is patient, love is kind. It does not envy, it does not boast, it is not proud. It does not dishonor others, it is not self-seeking, it is not easily angered, it keeps no record of wrongs. Love does not delight in evil but rejoices with the truth. It always protects, always trusts, always hopes, always perseveres. love never fails. (1 Cor. 13:4–8, New International Version)

The following will break down the biblical definition of love, which is agape love, into each component, will offer quotations from seminal thinkers, and will provide previous scholarly research and studies.

Love is patient. Love is having the ability not to quickly judge employees when they are not acting exactly as you think they should. Love is having the ability to not get agitated when situations do not go according to plans. Love is treating employees with the respect that they deserve as human beings, even when correction needs to be made. Being patient with ourselves when we fall short of our own expectations is also critical. Patience involves consistently working toward worthwhile goals and involves not getting discouraged when results do not come as anticipated. Love is patient with employees, and self, and knows that results come only with imperfect hard work and consistent dedication. Love is patient.

Love is kind. Love is treating every individual and situation from a position of kindness. Judish asserted that the concept of agape love started with the biblical commandment to love your neighbor as yourself (Judish, 1998). Judish also argued that neighborly love does not change based on the actions of others (Judish, 1998). Kindness is loving your neighbors, whether they be a physical neighbor, employee, or a coworker. Kindness is constant, firm, and unmoved. Harper found that love is demonstrated through the virtue of kindness, as possessed by a leader (Harper, 2017).

Every individual has worth that is not determined by social, hierarchical, or economic status. How you treat an individual is based on basic respect for all humanity, all of which deserve kindness. The researcher argues that leaders tend to regret any act of unkindness and tend to experience contentment with any act of kindness. Even when a supervisor delivers bad news to an employee it is done from a position of kindness and is usually done in private. Love is kind.

Love does not envy. Love is possessing the ability to be happy for coworkers, and employees when they succeed or when something good happens to them. Love involves; not, metaphorically, sucking on a sour lemon every time you hear of someone who has achieved much, fallen into good luck, or is blessed in some way. Possessing envy results in being continuously miserable because good things will always be happening to others. Ridding oneself of envy can result in feelings of contentment and goodwill toward all men and women. Love rejoices when an employee has achieved much, love rejoices when a work associate falls into good luck, and love rejoices when anyone is blessed in some way. Love does not envy.

Love does not boast. Love is possessing the ability not to tell others excessively of your achievements, good fortunes, and abilities. Harper stated that love, as demonstrated through humility, plays a role in the relationship development between leader and employee (Harper, 2017). The researcher contends that employees tend to respect a leader who is humble regarding his or her achievements, good fortunes, and abilities. The researcher would also say that leaders who do not boast tend to look to lift and praise others, often and frequently, without focusing on themselves. Boasting is not required for peers or employees to recognize a leader's success. Good works will produce a result that will be respected and appreciated by others without boasting to others. Love does not boast.

Love is not proud. Love does not elevate him or herself

above others. Pride usually starts with boasting about achievements, good fortunes, or abilities, and ends with feelings of superiority, therefore, I am better than you. Love elevates others, and a leader with love does not believe that one is elevated by knocking others down. Humility is the opposite of pride. Proverbs states the following: "Pride goeth before destruction, and an haughty spirit before a fall. Better it is to be of an humble spirit" (Prov. 16:18–19, King James Version). Harper found that humility was a recurring theme of love empowered leaders. Harper found that humility in a leader, as reported by participants, contributes to leadership effectiveness (Harper, 2017). Love is not proud.

Love does not dishonor others. Love is having the

ability not to engage in activities that bring dishonor to employees, present or not. Dishonoring employees can happen in the following ways: backbiting, gossiping, teasing, degrading others in any way, or shaming. Harper found that love is displayed through the honoring of others, placing value on everyone, regardless of position or rank within the hierarchy (Harper, 2017). Love honors others and does not engage in unbecoming activities that lead to the intentional or unintentional infliction of pain or embarrassment on an employee. Harper asserted that when a leader has an issue that arises, the love-empowered leader approaches the situation from a standpoint of love, takes the time to explain, and presents the information in a positive manner (Harper, 2017). Love lifts others to a higher level of living, expresses appreciation, and honors others. Love does not dishonor others.

Love is not self-seeking. Love is having the ability to look outside of yourself and be selfless toward others. Chang and Mansford pointed to the biblical event of when Jesus washed the feet of his disciples (John 13, King James Version) as an event where Christ expressed his love through serving and unselfishness (Chang & Mansford, 2016). Takaaki asserted that love is shown through the service of others (Takaaki, 2014). The opposite of selfishness, the selfless leader seeks to meet the needs of those around him or her. The researcher proclaims that being selfless tends to lead to increased happiness, and an increased sense of worth for both the leader and the employee. This happiness results from a focus on others, and not a focus on oneself. Having a genuine interest in the long-term development and success of others is also part of not self-seeking. Love is not self-seeking.

Love is not easily angered. Love does not frequently become angry. The Bible states: "He that is slow to anger is better than the mighty; and he that ruleth his spirit than he that taketh a city" (Prov. 16:32, King James Version). The researcher maintains that very few good outcomes come as a result of being angry. When a leader loses control of his or her emotions, the leader is at risk of saying or acting in a way that causes harm to an employee. The opposite of anger is love, calm, serenity, peace, and forgiveness. An individual who possesses love knows that the fruits of anger are broken relationships, and that the fruits of love are healed relationships. Leaders have control over their emotions and can address a difficult situation without letting their emotions hijack their ability to problem solve without anger. Love is not easily angered.

Love keeps no record of wrongs. Love includes taking the time to notice, acknowledge, and build upon the strengths of others, while at the same time being able to overlook their shortcomings. Focusing on the positive, and not dwelling on the negative, can lead to increased relational happiness and productivity. This also includes being able to let go of past mistakes and being able to fully live in the present. Chang and Mansford assert that love is to be extended to all, even enemies (Chang & Mansford, 2016). Holding on to grudges from the past, or not loving enemies, acts as a poison for relationships. Letting go of the past, and forgiving others, can result in the healing of relationships, and frees the leader to speak his or her mind and will. Making mental lists of the shortcomings of employees results in misery for the list maker. Love makes lists of the strengths of employees and builds upon those strengths. Love lets go of the bad and clings to the good. Love keeps no record of wrongs.

Love does not delight in evil. Love is inherently not

evil. Love is the opposite of evil. This includes being a proponent for the good of employees, helping employees get up when they fall, and helping employees avoid painful mistakes. Halter asserted that agape love leadership is a way for leaders to truly help others in a healthy and holistic manner (Halter, 2006). There is no delight when others make mistakes, only a desire to help individuals move onward and upward from mistakes. Love sees mistakes as an opportunity to learn and adjust future actions. Love makes proactive choices and actions to avoid the temptation of evil for oneself and employees. Love feels sorrow for oneself or others when evil is chosen. Love rejects evil and protects oneself and others from its snares. Love does not delight in evil.

Love rejoices with the truth. Love involves being genuine and sincere with others. Being fake, insincere, controlling, manipulative, or deceptive with others would be the opposite of rejoicing with the truth. Love gives the leader the ability to develop an employee through positive coaching through telling the truth in a way that is forward looking. Grossi asserted that love helps individuals find what is right and true in a situation (Grossi, 2016). Harper declared that love provides a safe environment where truth and protection are given (Harper, 2017). Living truthfully within ourselves, and with others, can result in greater, more meaningful relationships. Living truthfully also can make life simpler, because lies and deceptions do not need to be kept track of. Rejoicing and encouraging others when they are sincere, exhibit honesty, and are genuine is critical. Love rejoices when the truth is followed and chosen by oneself and others. Love seeks truth wherever truth is found and shares this truth with others to lift and inspire. Love rejoices with the truth.

Love always protects. Love is guarding and protecting those with whom you have responsibility over. Leaders have stewardship over those that they have been entrusted. Stewardship involves making sure that the needs of others that you care for are being met. Love is making sure that they are being treated fairly and making sure they are making strides forward with their personal and professional growth. It gives great comfort to individuals when they know that their steward is looking after their needs. Love always protects.

Love always trusts. Love includes extending trust to employees to show that you have confidence in their decisions, abilities, and efforts. Micromanagement is the opposite of always trusting. Harper asserted that like trust, love extends empowerment (Harper, 2017). Harper found in a phenomenological qualitative study that love-driven leaders extend trust to others, allow them to pursue passions, and enable them to fulfill their destinies (Harper, 2017). Extending and accepting trust can create a work environment that is free, innovative, and open to change. When a leader extends trust, employees feel like they can make decisions, in good faith, without being reprimanded. The researcher alleges that when employees know that a leader trusts them, their confidence in their abilities increase, and the result is in an increase in productivity. The leader sets the stage regarding creating an environment of trust. If a leader displays distrust in employees, and is micromanaging, the employee can begin to feel imprisoned, display low productivity, and may even begin to look elsewhere for work. Extending trust and accepting trust from other co-workers is critical to having a healthy and productive work environment. Love always trusts.

Love always hopes. Love displays optimism in the

efforts and abilities of others. Hoping for the best is a characteristic of great leaders. People generally do not like to work with a leader who is constantly complaining and not hopeful. On the other hand, working with an individual who is positive, uplifting, and hopeful can be very enjoyable. The researcher claims that the mood and temperament of leaders can be contagious, and when a leader displays a cheerful, hopeful attitude, this attitude can have a direct effect on improving the attitudes of employees. Love always hopes.

Love always perseveres. Love involves the ability of a leader to persevere through hard and difficult circumstances. Harper found in a qualitative study that perseverance was an emergent theme from the study of a love-driven leader (Harper, 2017). Most things in life that are worthwhile involve working through hard and difficult circumstances. Great leaders know how to work hard and get through the hard times. They know that on the other side of persevering is triumph and glory. This also involves helping employees persevere through their difficult life situations, both at work and in their personal life. Businesses and individuals go through the ups and downs of the business cycle, and persevering through the troughs of this cycle is critical for long term success. Love never gives up; love always perseveres.

Love never fails. Paul in his writings to the Corinthians

gives the bold assertion that love never fails (1 Cor. 13:8, The New

King James Version), and later counsels that all things be done in

love (1 Cor. 16:14, The New King James Version). Incorporating

love into leadership adds a leadership component that has the

potential of making a significant difference in the lives of people and

the organizations they represent. Approaching sensitive leadership

situations, with a true desire to do what is best for others, can help

resolve complicated situations. Leaders can have confidence in their

actions when love is the motivator because love never fails.

Studies

Grossi examined the role of love in law and found that the

two are interconnected. Grossie found that love gives law flexibility

to adapt to individual circumstances. Organizations have company

policies that can be compared to the law and inserting love in a

similar manner can give the flexibility to adapt the company policies

to individual circumstances. Grossi also concluded that Christian

love is for Christians, and that romantic love is for intimate relationships. He asserted that there needs to be another type of love that can be utilized for all, and this is a friendship love (Grossi, 2016).

Ricciardi found in a correlational study, that examined love and servant leadership, that the perceived leadership ability of servant leaders is positively correlated with the perceived love the leader demonstrates toward followers. Leaders who possess the characteristics of love are perceived by followers as having a higher leadership ability than a leader who does not possess love (Ricciardi, 2014).

Chang and Mansford completed a comparative study of agape love and Confucian Ren and concluded that agape love and Confucian Ren can both be used to help create a more ecumenical world (Chang & Mansford, 2016). Along the same line of thinking, Greenleaf stated that the application of servant leadership leads to a more just and caring world (Greenleaf, 1977).

Halter conducted a study in which he surveyed participants before and after a three-day seminar regarding agape leadership. Halter found, after statistical analysis, that participants had an increase in agape leadership characteristics following the seminar.

Teaching others about agape leadership results in an increase in its
characteristics among those who are taught (Halter, 2006).

Harper, in a phenomenological qualitative study of a love-
empowered leader, found the following as emergent themes from the
participant interviews: humility, honor, kindness, trust,
empowerment, wisdom, and perseverance (Harper, 2017).

Dierendonck and Patterson, in a study that integrated
previous studies and research regarding compassionate love and
servant leadership, found that when a leader demonstrates
compassionate love, other virtuous traits are encouraged in the
leader, such as forgiveness, humility, gratitude, and altruism
(Dierendonck & Patterson, 2015). The virtuous traits of the servant
leader encourage the servant leader to practice servant principles,
such as empowerment, authenticity, providing direction, and
stewardship. Dierendonck asserted that the result of a servant leader
demonstrating compassionate love, virtuous traits, and servant
leadership principles are the following: increased follower well-
being, optimal human functioning, meaningfulness, and a sense of
community (Dierendonck & Patterson, 2015).

Self found in an intertexture analysis of love as spoken in First Corinthians 13 in the Holy Bible that love has evolved into a viable form of leadership. Self asserted that there is a need for a more biblical, loving approach to leadership in order to deal with the ethical complexities in the, what is now, business environment. Self argued that agape is a love that is active and accomplishes goals and objectives. Self professed that leaders will constantly fail in applying the principle of love in leadership, because we all fail, but what is required is leaders who are willing to learn from their mistakes, and continually come back to the foundation of leadership founded on love (Self, 2009).

Goodier and Eisenberg found in an exploratory study of love in First Corinthians that leadership founded on love is a leadership that must meet others in a way that is meaningful. Goodier and Eisenberg also found in the analysis that Paul went against the norm in society by suggesting that all things be done in love (Goodier & Eisenberg, 2006).

Nishii found when interviewing 15 servant leaders across America that the participants were focused on others, and that this focus on others came because of possessing. Nishii found that servant leaders, and the love that they show employees, customers, and the organization, are often not recognized within organizations. Leadership within many organizations is often masculine, tough, and hypercompetitive, and servant leadership and love are often viewed as feminine and foreign within the organizational leadership culture. Nishii found that love as demonstrated through servant leadership is often misunderstood in the leadership of organizations, even though servant leadership is a widely accepted leadership philosophy by professionals, scholars, and practitioners (Nishii, 2017).

Servant Leadership

Servant leadership is a theory that proclaims that leadership is about serving those over whom the leader has stewardship over. Zentner found that the following religions of the world have core values that are consistent with the values of servant leadership: Buddhism, Christianity, Confucianism, Hinduism, Islam, Jainism, Judaism, Shinto, Sikhism, Taoism, and Zoroastrianism (Zentner, Aeron. 2015). Jesus Christ stated: "But he that is greatest among you shall be your servant" (Matt. 23:11, King James Version). Servant leadership was introduced into the business realm by Robert K.

Greenleaf, after a 40-year management career with AT&T, with his 1977 article titled *Servant Leadership: A Journey into the Nature of Legitimate Power and Greatness*. Greenleaf wrote:

> A new moral principle is emerging which holds that the only authority deserving one's allegiance is that which is freely and knowingly granted by the leader in response to, and in proportion to, the clearly evident servant stature of the leader (Greenleaf, 1995).

Greenleaf asserted that leaders are servants first, and then aspire to lead. Serving first was very important to Greenleaf. The leader who aspires to lead first has different motivations than the leader who is servant first (Greenleaf, 1977). Servant leaders are to serve the needs of the employees and customers first in a selfless way. Chung argued that the reason that leaders should adopt servant leadership into their practice is because the core value of servant leadership is to love other people (Chung, 2011).

Mani claimed that Jesus Christ created leadership development practices of servant leadership over two thousand years ago that are considered the latest leadership strategies of the twenty-first century (Mani, 2015). Greenleaf stated the following regarding how to measure the effects of servant leadership:

> The best test, and difficult to administer, is: Do those served grow as persons? Do they, while being served, become healthier, wiser, freer, more autonomous, more likely themselves to become servants? And, what is the effect on the least privileged in society? Will they benefit or at least not be further deprived? (Greenleaf, 1977).

Coetzer, Bussin, and Geldenhuys found in comparative literature review of servant leadership that it has a positive correlation with employee performance and employee organizational commitment (Coetzer, Bussin, & Geldenhuys, 2017). Nishii found that servant leaders see a higher purpose for both employees and the organizations for which they serve (Nishii, 2017). Laub (1999) defined servant leadership as:

> Servant leadership is an understanding and practice of leadership that places the good of those led over the self-interest of the leader. Servant leadership promotes the valuing and development of people, the building of community, the practice of authenticity, the providing of

leadership for the good of those led, and the sharing of power

and status for the common good of each individual, the total

organization, and those served by the organization. (Laub,

1999)

Characteristics of Servant Leaders

Focht and Ponton found over 100 characteristics of servant

leadership in the academic literature, and through a Delphi study

were able to narrow it down to the following 12 characteristics of

servant leaders: valuing people, humble, listening, trusting, caring,

having integrity, serving, empowering, serving others' needs before

their own, collaborating, loving unconditionally, and learning (Focht

& Ponton, 2015). The following literature review will break down

the characteristics of servant leadership as found in the research of

Focht and Ponton and will provide a review of research and studies

within the topic of servant leadership.

Value people. People are at the heart of servant

leadership. People are the most important aspect of the business to

the servant leader. Making, keeping, and improving relationships with all employees in the business, regardless of position, is of utmost importance (Parris & Peachey, 2013). All employees have value and deserve to be treated as such. Hodoh found in a correlational study that there is a positive relationship between servant leaders valuing their people and employee productivity (Hodoh, 2016). Jit, Sharma, and Kawatra asserted that because servant leaders value people, they are better able to lift employees out of emotional turmoil and to build an emotionally healthy and competitive workforce (Jit, Sharma, & Kawatra, 2017). The servant leader values people, respects them, and handles them with the care of a steward over his or her stewardship. Servant leaders value their people and elevate them to their greatest potential in life and organizational effectiveness. George (2003) stated the following about the importance of leaders developing enduring relationships with followers:

> The capacity to develop close and enduring relationships is one mark of a leader. Unfortunately, many leaders...believe their job is to create strategy, structure and processes....This detached style of leadership will not be successful in the 21st century.

Servant leaders take the time to build and keep relationships as well as create strategy, structure, and processes. It is not one or the other. It is both. Production and processes are not hurt because the leader is a servant. The researcher asserts that all areas are strengthened when a leader values the people in the organization. Servant leaders value people.

Humility. Servant leaders are humble; they do not boast of their own strength. If they have accomplished or are accomplishing great things, they keep it to themselves, and let their actions and results speak for them. They are quick to praise in public, slow to judge, and know that they do not have all the answers. Accepting and implementing constructive criticism is easier for the servant leader, because of humility. Harper found in a phenomenological qualitative study of love-empowered leaders that when leaders possess humility then transparency is also present. Harper avouched that leaders with humility are open and willing to share the ups and downs of their own story, without being worried about how people think of them (Harper, 2017). Harper found that humility is a trait of a leader that sets the employees at ease in his or her presence (Harper, 2017). Servant leaders possess humility.

Listening. Taking the time to listen to employees is very important to the servant leader. Employees have emotional needs that must be met for employees to be productive and happy. Listening to employees helps the servant leader to discover and meet these emotional needs. Burden (2014) asserted that most individuals are selective listeners, and that servant leaders should be empathetic listeners who set aside bias and take time to empathetically listen to employees. It is said that employees do not care how much you know until they know how much you care, and a leader shows how much he or she cares about employees by taking the time to listen to them. Servant leaders listen.

Trust. Servant leaders know when it is smart to extend trust to employees, and they follow through when trust is extended to them. Trust helps bind all the business relationships together. Servant leaders are men and women of their word. When they commit to doing something, it is considered a very high priority, and it is done. Making and keeping commitments is based on the mutual trust of both the leader and the follower. Servant leaders also hold employees accountable regarding trust. They keep a high standard of trust and teach and train employees to keep this standard. Trusting also allows the servant leader not to be involved in every detail of the business. The employees of a servant leader know when trust has been extended, and they feel comfortable taking initiative on a project. Servant leaders extend trust and are trusted.

Caring. Servant leaders care about the well-being of their employees. Servant leaders are to some extent healers because they seek to improve the lives of the employees that are entrusted to their care. Proverbs states that what is desired in man is kindness (Prov. 19:22, The New King James Version). All employees are facing their own struggles in life, and having a leader who cares, is invested in you, and wants to facilitate your success, can facilitate the employee's development. Helping employees overcome obstacles in their life elevates them, lifts their burdens, frees their minds, and makes them more able to be productive workers. Employee career development can be facilitated through the servant leader taking the time to care for his or her employees. Servant leaders are caring.

Integrity. Servant leaders have integrity and expect

integrity from employees under his or her care. Integrity is a

characteristic that can take a long time to gain, and something that

can be lost in an instant. When a servant leader has integrity, he or

she can have a clean heart, clean hands, and clear mind. When a

servant leader has integrity, he or she can speak with a clear mind,

and direct others within the framework of integrity. Integrity helps to

build the trust of employees, and employees can look to the leader as

an example. Servant leaders that have integrity help to build the

reputation of the business and add to the long-term value of the

organization. Servant leaders possess integrity.

Service. Greenleaf (1977) stated servant leaders are

servants first before they even think about being a leader. Only after

an individual is fully a servant of others can the servant aspire to

lead others through service. Serving others is the most important

aspect of servant leadership, and it is how servant leaders show their

love for their employees. Nishii (2017) asserted that the servant

leader's ability to be selfless comes from within.

The service of servant leaders extends beyond individual followers or employees. Servant leaders serve all the stakeholders of the organization. Ebener and O'Connell (2010) asserted that servant leaders encourage others to go above and beyond their immediate interests by serving the needs of the organization. Organizational citizenship behaviors are demonstrated and encouraged by servant leaders. Servant leaders feel a stewardship for individual followers, for the customers, and for the organization. Servant leaders can find the proper balance of serving the needs of all the stakeholders in the organization. Servant leaders serve others.

Empowering. Servant leaders are experts at empowering employees. Tanno (2017) found in a phenomenological study that all 18 participants agreed that servant leaders empower their employees. Linuesa-Langreo, Ruiz-Palomino, and Elche found in a comparative case study of servant leadership in the hospitality industry that servant leaders create an organizational climate that empowers employees, and that an empowering climate creates a more creative workforce (Linuesa-Langreo, Ruiz-Palomino, & Elche, 2016). Empowerment involves extending smart trust to employees.

Employees of servant leaders are not in a constant state of fear of their leader looking over their shoulder. They are also not in fear of their leader criticizing them for taking initiative on a project or task. Servant leaders do not see taking initiative as a mistake, even if a mistake is made. Servant leaders have the unique ability to see everything that happens, can overlook trivial mistakes, can correct an employee in a positive way, and has the foresight to encourage employees frequently. Servant leaders empower employees.

Serve others' needs before their own. Servant

leaders are constantly looking for opportunities to serve their employees. Selfless service is the highest priority of the servant leader. The servant leader is not concerned about self but is concerned about serving employees, customers, and other stakeholders. This is an elevated view of leadership. Servant leaders who serve their employees first are generally more happy leaders to be around. This is because they can remove the focus from self through the service of others. Nishii, when interviewing 15 servant leaders, found that they chose to be servant leaders even though they knew that it was against the leadership grain of the organization. The servant leader participants often preferred to serve the needs of others in the organization behind the scenes, or quietly when no one was watching. Serving the needs of others was their focus, and they did not want recognition for it (Nishii, 2017). For example, Mike, a senior executive servant leader in Nishii's study stated the following:

A truly great servant leader, nobody knows how you're helping them. When you're doing it right, it's not a celebration of you. It's a recognition that your job is to be of service to those people who work on your team and support them. And that to me is very fulfilling, when you're in a role and you know intrinsically that you did something that helps people.

Collaboration. Servant leaders know that they do not know everything, and that the power of two working together is much stronger than two working individually. Humility plays a large part in the servant leader being willing to collaborate and work with others. The servant leader is willing to listen to new ideas, to be corrected when needed, and is willing to implement the ideas of others. Tanno found in a phenomenological study that all interview participants perceived taking the time to listen to the ideas of others as a component of what makes servant leadership an effective leadership model (Tanno, 2017).

Love (unconditional love). Servant leaders

demonstrate unconditional love toward employees, customers, and other leaders. Individuals show they care when service is given for the benefit of others. When a leader shows love to employees, he or she cares about the past, present, and future well-being of the individual. A servant leader can show his or her love for employees by helping them with their professional development. Love can also be shown by holding employees to high standards of conduct and productivity. Servant leaders do not see the elevation of others professionally as a threat. Instead, the servant leader helps elevate the careers of others and expects their best efforts. Loving an employee does not mean that the servant leader is soft with employees. For example, a coach on a football team may be hard on some of the players because he or she loves the players and wants them to grow in their capacities and performance. Correction, and the continual improvement of employees, is implemented because the servant leader loves his or her employees. Love is the motivator that powers the actions performed in servant leadership. Servant leaders serve because of love. Servant leaders develop employees because of love. Servant leaders encourage employee improvement because of love. Servant leaders excel in the business world because of love. Servant leaders possess love for others.

Learning. Servant leaders are not stagnant when it comes to learning. Learning is a part of their leadership routine. Dickson argued that lifelong learning is an essential characteristic of successful individuals, and can also lead to health benefits (Dickson, 2008). Dickson also asserted that lifelong learning is essential for leaders to keep up with the continuous changes in the world economy (Dickson, 2008). The servant leader who is not continually learning is a leader that is falling behind. Servant leaders are continually looking for ways to improve themselves and lift those who surround them. Love of learning throughout a lifetime is part of the servant leadership success pattern. Servant leaders are continually learning.

Studies

Linuesa-Langreo, Ruiz-Palomino, and Elche conducted a comparative case study analysis of servant leaders in the hospitality industry and found that when servant leadership is present in a work group, high levels of group empowerment and group creativity emerge. The study also found that when empowerment is present in a work climate, creativity is also present (Linuesa-Langreo, Ruiz-Palomino, & Elche, 2016).

Jit, Sharma, and Kawatra conducted a qualitative study that explored how servant leaders, empathize, understand, and address the emotional turmoil of employees through emotional healing. Semi-structured interviews were conducted with 15 servant leaders, and it was found that servant leaders contribute to an emotionally healthy workforce, which can facilitate a competitive advantage for the organization. It was found that servant leaders can listen, empathize, and assist employees out of emotional turmoil. Because servant leaders are characteristically apt to serve others, they are more inclined to help and assist employees in emotional need (Jit, Sharma, & Kawatra, 2017).

Davis conducted a qualitative correlational study in which the variables of self-transcendence and servant leadership were under examination. Davis found that there is a strong correlation between self-transcendence or spirituality and servant leadership. In other words, the more spiritual a leader is, the more apt the leader is to lead in a servant leadership style. Davis also found that the self-declared servant leaders in the study ranked prayer fulfillment highest on the Assessment of Spirituality of Religious Sentiments Scale (Davis, 2014).

Coetzer, Bussin, and Geldenhuys conducted a systematic literature review of servant leadership to identify the functions, objectives, characteristics, and core competencies of servant leaders. The study identified the following characteristics of servant leaders: authenticity, humility, compassion, accountability, courage, altruism, integrity, and listening. The study found the following to be strong core competencies of servant leaders: empowerment, stewardship, building relationships, and compelling vision. The results of the study also indicated a negative correlation between servant leadership and employee burnout, and a negative correlation between servant leadership and employee turnover intention.

Employees that are led by servant leaders experience less burnout and have a lower turnover rate (Coetzer, Bussin, & Geldenhuys, 2017).

Tanno conducted a phenomenological study in which he conducted interviews with high level executives who were self-declared servant leaders of organizations that used servant leadership in their business model. Tanner found that the servant leaders saw themselves as stewards over both their people and the organization which they represented. The servant leaders served customers, employees, the organization, and stakeholders. The themes found in the study were the following: serve and steward others, spiritual wholeness, business ethics, empowerment, build community, communication, and teamwork (Tanno, 2017). Tanno stated the following regarding the theme of teamwork:

> The one structure of experience that prevailed throughout this study is teamwork. The meaning of teamwork is analogous to the functioning family. The family in a servant leadership organization has a leader, the Primus, who knows the way, fosters an environment of serving others needs first and stewardship of time, talent, treasure, and the

organization. Decisions are made ethically with other family members for the common good. The members of the family are empowered to become the best they can be and mentored to do good works within the family community and the greater community. The community is an extension of the family where alliances and partnerships are made to thrive and to build a better world. (Tanno, 2017)

Nishii conducted a Heideggerian hermeneutic study in which 15 servant leaders were interviewed regarding their experiences as servant leaders. Nishii found that the participants of the study were caring, kind, and nice, but that their caring was not about being nice. Nishii found that the servant leader participants showed that they care by giving followers challenges such as leap-ahead care, tough love, and empowerment (Nishii, 2017).

Nishii also found that the servant leader participants often found themselves with internal conflicts when serving both the needs of employees and the needs of the organization (Nishii, 2017). This often occurs when it is necessary to terminate an employee because of low productivity. Nishii found that servant leaders focus more on improving individuals within the organization, and that transformational leaders tend to focus more on improving the organization. The servant leaders focused on the higher needs of the employees and the higher purpose of the organization (Nishii, 2017).

Martinez conducted a qualitative, grounded, inductive, and interpretive case study in which 14 servant leaders, at various leadership levels, from multiple congregations in The Church of Jesus Christ of Latter-day Saints were interviewed. The aim of the study was to explore how the servant leaders developed servant leadership characteristics over time and within the Restored Church of Jesus Christ's framework. It was found that serving as a missionary acted as a "boot camp" in servant leadership training, and that the experiences of a missionary lay the foundation for a life as a servant leader. It was also found that The Church intentionally provides a leadership model that is patterned after Christ's leadership model. The leadership training of the Church focuses on serving others in the Savior's way. Because there are no paid positions within the congregations, all positions are viewed as serving others. The leadership mentors, leadership training, and continual leadership opportunities within The Church of Jesus Christ of Latter-day Saints facilitate the nurturing and growth of servant leaders (Martinez, 2016).

In a study that explored servant leader traits from the life of Jesus, Chung found the following traits: humility, obedience to God, team building, and relationship among, not over others (Chung, 2011). Chung summed up the study with the following:

To be a servant leader following the example of Jesus is neither easy nor natural. It requires hard training and continuous exercise. It is not a matter of skills or capability but a matter of the heart and perception. It is contrary to the self-centered tendencies of humankind. Consequently, servant leaders should seek to emulate Jesus; serving others is the example that Jesus left for His followers. He abandoned all that He had before He came to this earth: glory, adoration, power, authority, comfort, and even creatorship. Humility and sacrifice marked the path that Jesus took, which in turn placed Him to the right hand of God. Love made it all possible. (Chung, 2011)

Lorence conducted a quantitative, non-experimental, predictive study regarding the statistical predictive relationship between servant leadership and perceived effective leadership. Employees in non-leadership roles in for-profit organizations were surveyed, and it was revealed that a strong statistical predictive relationship exists between the constructs of servant leadership and effective leadership. The following servant leadership characteristics were found to have a predictive correlation with effective leadership: stewardship, interpersonal acceptance, empowerment, humility, and authenticity. The study found followers perceived servant leaders as effective leaders (Lorence, 2018).

Mani (2015) conducted a review of how Jesus Christ approached leadership development as written in the Bible. Mani found that Christ did the following: Inspired/invited others to join something with purpose greater than themselves, appealed to the disciples desire for growth and development, chose humble ordinary men that were willing to trust and learn, chose disciples who had different talents and abilities, taught others through leading by example, was willing to spend quality time to teach, train, and lift, demonstrated the importance of stewardship of others, developed others through teaching truth, taught using parables or stories with powerful life lessons, was patient when teaching important

principles, empowered others through the delegation of
responsibility, held others accountable, was direct when enlisting the
help of others, and did not shy away from giving corrective feedback
when needed. Mani asserted that Christ did not give attention to
qualifications and talents but to honesty and character, and that
Christ's leadership model of servant leadership is now considered
the new leadership model of the twenty-first century (Mani, 2015).

Ebener and O'Connell conducted a qualitative case study of
three individual high performing parishes and found that servant
leadership was also accompanied by high-organizational citizenship
behaviors. The personal care given by the servant leaders often
translated into organizational citizenship behaviors. Ebener and
O'Connell also found that service was contagious, and that service
was often reciprocated after it was received (Ebener & O'Connell,
2010). Ebener and O'Connell stated the following in the concluding
remarks:

The servant leader is more inclined to serve than to be
served, recognize rather than to be recognized, and empower
rather than to flex positional power by commanding and
controlling the response of followers. If leaders place

themselves in humble service to their organization, recognize the gifts and talents of others, and call them forth through empowering actions, then the people will respond with organizational citizenship behaviors by helping each other, taking initiative, participating in various activities, and taking responsibility to continuously develop themselves as potential leaders of their organizations. (Ebener & O'Connell, 2010)

Hodoh conducted a quantitative correlational study in which he researched if there was a correlation between employee-perceived servant leadership and employee productivity. A total of 133 employees from three high performing distribution centers of a national supply chain participated in the study. The study revealed that there is a statistical positive correlation between the employee-perceived leaders' use of servant leadership and an increase in employee productivity. The study also revealed that there is a positive correlation between when servant leaders value their people and employee productivity (Hodoh, 2016).

The researcher utilized Academic Search Complete and Pro Quest Dissertations & Theses Full Text to conduct the literature review. Keywords utilized in the search included the following: love, agape, love and leadership, servant leadership, servant leader, and love and servant leadership.

Chapter 3: Methodology

This chapter details the statement of the problem, reviews the research questions that will be explored in the study, reviews the research methodology, reviews the research design, reviews the population and sample selection, describes the sources of data, reviews the validity of the data, reviews the reliability of the data, describes data collection procedures, describes data analysis procedures, reviews ethical considerations, and will conclude with the limitations of the study.

Statement of the Problem

This study examined the role of love in the leadership theory of servant leadership. Focht and Ponton found in a study that 86% of participants agreed, or strongly agreed, that love is a primary characteristic of servant leadership (Focht & Ponton, 2015). Ricciardi recommended future research on love and leadership effectiveness because of the link between love and leadership (Ricciardi, 2014). Rajek suggested that future research needs to be conducted regarding how love can be increased, and that this research should be infused into servant leadership development (Rajek, 2014). Sullivan recommended future research regarding love, forgiveness, and leadership (Sullivan, 2017). Harper recommended future research that focuses on love and leadership (Harper, 2017). Nishii recommended a phenomenological study with the topic including love and servant leadership (Nishii, 2017). The problem is a lack of research regarding the role of love in servant leadership.

Research Questions

Love and leadership are two terms that are not often associated with each other, although there seems to be a link between the two because the characteristics of love are often the characteristics of a good leader (Ricciardi, 2014). Love seems to fit nicely within the framework of servant leadership theory, since the main premise of servant leaders is to show love to employees through selfless service (Greenleaf, 1977). The following research questions were examined in an experiential context:

RQ1: What is the role of love in servant leadership?

RQ2: What do you think is the significance of love in today's leadership culture?

Research Methodology

Nishii stated the following:

> As I noted in my synthesizing reflection, the servant leaders dare to walk on the narrow ridge without clear answers or recipes to follow whether it is related to love, relationships, or power (or a combination of them). Further understanding of such experience through the phenomenological and hermeneutic approach would add value not only to the scholarly knowledge, but also to the practitioners of servant leadership. (Nishii, 2017)

The researcher followed this recommendation for future research by conducting a qualitative study and gathering real-life experience data for analysis. Because there is very little research that has combined love and servant leadership, a qualitative study, resulting in the exploration of the topic is suitable (Creswell, 2014).

Research Design

The research is qualitative in design and allowed the researcher to explore the complexities of the role of love in servant leadership. A quantitative study would not have allowed for an open exploration of the role of love in servant leadership. The researcher conducted semi-structured open-ended interviews with 10 self-declared servant leaders. The servant leader participants needed to have a total of at least five years of leadership experience.

The researcher aimed to achieve full data saturation through the data gathered in the study. Enough interviews were collected for themes to be easily extrapolated from the data. Data saturation was the measuring stick regarding how many participants were included in the study. The researcher is confident that an informationally representative sample resulted from a sample size of 10 participants.

Population and Sample Selection

The researcher utilized a snowball sampling method to find self-declared servant leaders for semi-structured interviews. A snowball sampling method was utilized because the participants needed to be servant leaders. The researcher found, contacted, and interviewed the first servant leader participant. The researcher then utilized the network of the first participant to locate, approach, and interview the second qualified participant. This referral process continued with each participant until enough interviews were scheduled and enough data was collected. Allowing participants to recruit and recommend participants who were servant leaders aided in finding the right participants. The total population was 100, the target population was 17, and the sample population was 10. The location was business leaders in their own environment located in Salt Lake County, Utah County, Wasatch County, Iron County, Washington County and Summit County in the State of Utah in the United States of America.

Sources of Data

All the data analyzed came from transcriptions from the semi-structured interviews of servant leaders. No other types of data were collected, included, or analyzed in the research. It was the intention of the researcher to exclude all other types of data, and to only include the interviews conducted by the researcher.

Validity

Creswell stated that social constructivists seek to understand the environments in which they live and work (Creswell, 2014). The ideas and beliefs of individuals come about through interactions with other individuals and through complex personal experiences. These personal experiences and interactions within an individual's environment aid in the construction of personal views. The questions in the interviews are very broad, and very general to allow for the participants to focus on their views and experiences regarding the role of love in servant leadership. The interviews encouraged the participants to explore the complexity of the topic, allowing for valid interviews with valuable data.

The researcher utilized inductive reasoning to look for trends or themes within the data, and then generalized the trends or themes. The researcher's main aim was to interpret and categorize the lived experiences of the participants. NVivo qualitative analysis software was utilized as a tool to extrapolate the trends and themes from the data. Utilizing NVivo helped to reduce the personal bias of the researcher from affecting the trend research.

Reliability

Seale asserted that when it comes to ensuring reliability in qualitative research that the participants need to be trustworthy (Seale, 1999). The researcher took the time to ensure that participants met the qualifications for the study and came with favorable recommendation from the referrer. The researcher also utilized reflexivity throughout the research process to aid in detecting and limiting personal bias throughout the research process. Darawsheh (2014) argues that utilizing reflexivity in qualitative research increases the rigor of the study. The researcher was introspective throughout the research process and was aware of personal biases that could influence the study. Being introspective regarding the effects of personal biases helped to bring the biases into light and helped the researcher formulate methods to help increase the reliability of the study (Smith, 2006).

Data Collection Procedures

Participants were asked to read and sign the informed consent form (Appendix A). Participants were assured that their privacy will be protected, and that private information would not be shared or made public. Interviews were recorded on a cassette recording device. All data collected was kept in a locked file and was only accessible by the researcher. Once the recorded interviews were transcribed, the cassettes were permanently destroyed via fire. All interview data that was made public or published is presented in a way that no information will make it possible to identify participants or affiliated companies. Coding was used to replace names to ensure the confidentiality of participants.

Data Analysis Procedures

The researcher utilized the interview guide, provided in Appendix B, to explore the research question of the role of love in servant leadership. Definitions of both servant leadership and agape love were presented to the participants, followed by open-ended questions that explored the role of love in servant leadership. The researcher then transcribed the recorded interviews, within two months, and analyzed the transcriptions using non-statistical analysis to analyze the data. NVivo qualitative data analysis software was used to comb through the transcriptions to find themes within the data. The researcher then organized the themes in the findings portion of the research. The research analysis aligned with the research design, because NVivo qualitative analysis software is used to effectively analyze qualitative studies, such as interviews.

Ethical Considerations

The researcher provided an informed consent form for each participant to read and sign. Confidentiality was provided to all participants in a way that all readers will not know the identity of each participant. Aliases/coding was utilized, and organizational names were not written. All interviews were recorded on the researcher's tape-recording device and were promptly destroyed via fire after transcription. The destruction of recordings happened within two months of transcription. All participants had the option of declining to participate in the study at any time, and without penalty.

The recordings were recorded on a handheld cassette tape recorder. The researcher destroyed the recorded tapes via fire after transcription occurred. The recorded interview tapes were destroyed within two months of recording. Transcriptions were held for a period of three years in a locked secure location where the researcher will be the only individual who will have access. After the three-year period the researcher will destroy transcriptions via fire.

Limitations

There are many limitations regarding the study that was conducted. One such limitation is that the results of the study cannot be generalized to include servant leaders in all organizations, because of the limited geographical area of the study. However, one could take the results of this study and compare it with other similar studies that have been, or will be, conducted in other geographic locations. Another limitation of this study is that the participants have personal biases that, in turn, may affect the results of the study. Participants may not take the time to honestly answer the questions, which could also limit the accuracy of the study results. There may be other research tools that could study the role of love in servant leadership in a more accurate way.

Summary

This chapter presented an overview of the qualitative study that examined the gap in the research regarding the role of love in the leadership theory of servant leadership. The following chapters will present the data, present the findings of the study, and present the recommendations as a result of the study.

Chapter 4: Data Analysis and Results

This chapter will begin with a narrative summary of the sample population, sample characteristics, and demographics. It includes graphic organizers to present coded data and concludes with the themes that were extrapolated from the interview data in a non-conclusionary manner.

Descriptive Data

The researcher contacted 17 servant leaders by phone to schedule interviews. From these contacts, 10 interviews were scheduled. 75 pages of interview data was transcribed and analyzed by NVivo qualitative data-analysis software on a question-by-question basis, as well as on the whole. Seven men and three women participated in the interviews. Four of the participants were top executives, three of the participants were successful entrepreneurs, one of the participants was a general manager, one of the participants was a small business owner, and one of the participants was a leader in a nonprofit organization.

Results

Figure 4.1 is an image showing the most-used words from the interviews regarding the role of love in servant leadership.

Figure 4.1 Participant Word Cloud

Figure 4.1. Role of love in servant leadership word cloud

Question 1.

In what ways do you see yourself as a leader who possesses love for others?

P7 shared the following:

You cannot lead unless you love. In my opinion, in my leadership approach, I am not a different person. I am true to who I am as a person. The way that I conduct my life is to try and love each individual. Whether it be family, business, friends, whatever it might be, I act with love first and foremost, at all times, in my leadership positions.

I do own my own business and have for 16 years. I try to put the person first always and try to love that person unconditionally. Even in moments of frustration or times where you think that they may not be conducting themselves the way you would like them too. I think that as an individual in a leadership position, if I do not respect the individual for who they are, and love them for who they are, then how can I possibly effectively lead them?

Even with our customers, I try very hard to understand them from their position, in our business relationship, so that the partnership can work, so that we can have mutual respect and love. Obviously, I do not tell my clients that I love them; there are boundaries certainly, but I find it critical in the way that I approach business, in the way that I treat them, that it reflects love. Especially with my team, it's a little bit easier to be a little warmer in that approach, because I want them to know that I love them, and I love their families. That is what I care about most is the well-being of them and their families, and that yes, work is important, but it is not the most important.

The most important thing, I believe, is our relationship with God, and then our relationship with our families. So, I try to create an environment that is safe, loving, and respectful, and where we can have a lot of fun and be passionate about what we do, because we love what we do. So that's the approach, and I find it to be a very important approach. I feel that you get the most out of people when they feel that they are important. They feel that they are respected when they feel that they are loved. I feel like they will give you their best, and the only way to do that is to lead by action. Words are empty. I can say whatever I want… So, I try to make my actions show that I truly love them regardless of any situation, that is first and foremost.

P8 shared the following:

I see myself as someone who really believes in people and their capabilities, for my employee's sake, because I believe we are all working together for the same goal, and if they feel appreciated, they will work harder. I specifically know that as I express love for them, or appreciation, they will reciprocate. Being a business owner is far more than just writing paychecks, it's being a leader, it's being a cheerleader, it's being a therapist, it's being everything. It's been an incredible experience to see my employees really come together as a group of people, who otherwise wouldn't be friends, who work really well together.

Table 4.1 presents the themes generated for question one through the utilization of NVivo qualitative analysis software.

Table 4.1

Question 1 Discovered Themes, Word Count, and Weighted Percentages

Themes	Word Count
Weighted Percentage	
1. People	37
2.13%	
2. Kindness	13
.75%	
3. Caring	11
.63%	
4. Appreciation	9
.52%	
5. Understanding	8
.46%	

Question 2.

What role does love play in servant leadership?

P2 shared the following:

It comes down to viewing those that we have a leadership role over in the same way we view the client or the end user of our product or service, as somebody who needs something. When I have had employees in the past, and I think that I have done this a differing level of success, if I view the employee in the same way that I have always tried to view the client, if I have fulfilled their needs properly, and if they can perceive that I care for them, as opposed to using them as a tool to get what I want, I have always felt like they perform better for me. Those employees that perceived me as a boss that was just using them as a means to enhance my own bottom line, I didn't feel that I could necessarily trust them, they must not have felt that they could trust me, and there was always an employee-employer relationship, more than those employees that I was able to successfully feel like we became partners, even though I may have been their boss.

P7 shared the following:

That is an interesting question because leading and managing can be two different things, or they can be completely intertwined. I have worked for people that their management style has been one of dictatorship, rather than one of leadership. I view leadership as leading by your actions, and hopefully, those actions reflect what you do and say. For me, servant leadership is an accurate description of how I approach leadership. I'm willing to serve my team, I'm willing to serve our customers in the same way that I expect my team to serve our customers. I don't expect them to do anything that I wouldn't do. I think that the only way you can do it, again it goes back to your core, and the core is that I love who I am associated with. I don't think you can dismiss it, at least for me, I cannot leave love out of a relationship with an individual. I might not like things that people do all the time, or decisions that people make, or decisions that my customers make, or my team makes, but at the end of the day, that must be separate from how I feel about them, and I love them no matter who they are.

I feel that if I can create that environment, we have an environment here where I feel that they love me, and they would do anything for me. Also, the reciprocal of that is because of respect, and it is not empty or hollow, it's true, and we live what we preach. I think as far as that goes with the servant leadership, and that theory, it goes back again to who your core is. That is, you are principled enough to know that the individual is what matters most, and hopefully love is the reaction.

Table 4.2 presents the themes generated for question 2 through the utilization of NVivo qualitative analysis software.

Table 4.2

Question Two Discovered Themes, Word Count, and Weighted Percentages

Themes	Word Count
Weighted Percentage	
1. People	21
1.57%	
2. Caring	18
1.35%	
3. Serve	18
1.35%	
4. Feeling	16
1.20%	
5. Relationships	10
.75%	

Question 3.

Is there anything that prevents you from utilizing love as a servant leader? If so, what?

P2 shared the following:

Well, I would say that I am not always great at developing that love, I told you I don't think it's necessarily a natural trait that I have, and I have to try to do it. Sometimes some people are harder to love than others, and if I were better at it, I think I could love those that are harder to love. But I have a harder time loving if I do not think that they were putting forward sufficient effort, or if they were not trustworthy. I owned a retail chain of outlets, and I found a lot of employees that would steal from me. It was hard for me to love. When somebody would steal, I found that I wasn't willing to work with them. If someone violated my trust, I was not willing to work with them. I would end the relationship, and I would find someone else that I felt I could trust.

P4 shared the following:

There are a couple of things: I think those things that would interfere with a servant leader would be the desire to be intimidating by those that are leading, or not trusting those that they are supposed to lead, and mistrust kills leadership. Also, a person that may not want to entertain the opinions of others. One of the reasons for a person being intimidated in a leadership position would be fearing those opinions or if somebody challenges something a leader might say, pride would not allow them to work with that person as effectively. They would use intimidation instead of love. They might use force, in a sense of saying something like, I'm the leader, you must do this. Instead of trying to find consensus or getting feedback.

So, I think pride would be something that would be an obstacle to leadership and fear in any position, we might have feared that people wouldn't want to do what I say, or the directive I might want to give, or need to give. Now if there is mutual trust and love, fear is something that I think is actually eliminated because you're seeking feedback. Letting one's own ego go, knowing that we are not always right, but if you have something you need to get done and approach people that you are leading, in a positive way, and they give something counter to what you are looking for as a response to your leadership, that might be a positive thing because it may be absolutely true what they are suggesting, and may work better. Then compromise enters that process and those people that a servant leader is asked to lead are much more willing because you entertain their feelings, and considered what they think, and actually treasure what they think. That's when things start to really have a positive effect in people's lives. Both the servant leader, the person you are called to lead, people just have a real synergy that wants to get things done because they know this person isn't full of ego or pride or fearful of the consequences if they're not followed, and how that person might be reprimanded even, and that's just no way to lead.

P5 shared the following:

I am not doing it because I want someone to know that I am doing it, and that's no simple task. Because it is so ingrained. I think that it is the biggest barrier. Even Mother Teresa certainly had a good PR campaign behind her. We just don't see doing good in the dark as leadership, if no one knows you are not leading. Consequently, it is hard to lead out of a godlike love, and certainly God does not get much credit.

Table 4.3 presents the themes generated for question 3 through the utilization of NVivo qualitative analysis software.

Table 4.3

Question 3 Discovered Themes, Word Count, and Weighted Percentages

Themes	Word Count
Weighted Percentage	
1. Differences	5
.48%	
2. Fear	5
.48%	
3. Stealing	5
.48%	
4. Lost Trust	5
.48%	
5. Competition	4
.38%	

Question 4.

What do you think is the significance of love in today's leadership culture?

P9 shared the following:

I don't think people put enough significance on it. I think that too many people feel that there's not a place for love in today's leadership, and I think that's the problem with society. I think businesses would run better, schools would run better, government would run better, everything would run better if people would take this approach. I think there are too many people that feel that in leadership, if you are showing love, that it shows weakness, and they are wrong.

P3 shared the following:

I think that it's not as significant as it once was. I think that loyalty in a company, people change jobs a lot more often, the younger generation doesn't really have the same work ethic as a lot of the older people have. I think that a lot of it is a lot more impersonal. I think we are less impersonal as we have our systems of communications. Texting has made us a lot less impersonal as a society, and yet we can't be all business either. You have to have that personal touch and I feel that when people know that you care about them, I think you can create that loyalty and when certain people and certain bosses or employees, so to speak, have all the arrows pointing inward, it's all about them, it's all about their time, all about their job, and those that have the arrows pointing outward, where you are concerned about others, and the conversation is outward. It is a job, and we need to do it the best we can. If we have the support of each other, and the care for each other, I think that there's a lot of mileage in it for the institution.

Table 4.4 presents the themes generated for question 4 through the utilization of NVivo qualitative analysis software.

Table 4.4

Question 4 Discovered Themes, Word Count, and Weighted Percentages

Themes	Word Count
Weighted Percentage	
1. People	30
2.82%	
2. Feeling	15
1.32%	
3. Different	10
.94%	
4. Better	8
.75%	
5. World	7
.66%	

Question 5.

Have you found yourself in a particular situation where a leader was needed who possessed great love for others? If so, could you please explain the situation and how it was handled?

P6 shared the following:

We had a guy in production, he had been with us for three years, recovering alcoholic, and multiple felonies. He had been dry for one year when we hired him. He had kept his nose clean, so to speak, he had a couple of kids, and we decided to give him a chance. For the first time in his life, he was actually taking responsibility for his life. He did great for a year or two, doing great, hard worker, bright as the morning sun, smart guy, doing a great job, a fun-loving guy, and he put a firecracker in the women's restroom, under the toilet seat. So, when our office manager sat down it went off. It traumatized her, we had to pay for counseling for months.

She couldn't go outside to see the fireworks on the Fourth of July. To her, it just traumatized her. I called our attorney and asked what I have to do legally? He said, legally you are probably better off to let him go. However, if this is his first offense, for something like that, and you do not think that this woman is going to sue you, you are probably OK if you keep him. It was a tough decision.

We had this woman who had been with us at that time for eight years, doing a great job, and she felt a little betrayed that we did not fire him instantly. On the other hand, we have a guy who is on his third year of being clean and criminal free. He could not even drive at this time, his wife had to drop him off at work. You know, what does this do to him if we fire him? So, between counsel from attorneys, and board members we decided to try and work with him.

We had some pretty frank discussions with him, and he realized that he had probably crossed the line in today's world. When you were a kid this would not have meant anything, but today it was pretty serious. I think that the final decision was driven by love, by concern for the individual, and he is now our production manager. He is still dry, is still clean, he has four kids now, and is doing great. He is acting responsible, and his kids are attending church with his mother. The progress is incredible. I mean, he is a great asset now. He is absolutely dependable and will do anything to do what he needs to do for the business or for me personally. He is just a great asset. I shudder to think that we were on a razor's edge whether to fire him or not. The office manager ended up quitting a year or two later because she wanted to become a stay-at-home mom, and we were excited for her to be able to do that. We won. It wasn't an easy thing to do, but it was driven on who he was, what his history was, and what it might do to his family. He stepped up and it was a good decision.

P8 shared the following:

I was very involved with sports while growing up and I had a volleyball coach in junior high. She had an incredible ability to be a leader. She brought us all together who otherwise wouldn't necessarily be friends. She gave us a cause, and it was totally outside of volleyball. She challenged us to not drink soda for the season of volleyball. Well that turned into this whole friendship thing that went all the way through high school for some of us. She also had these motivational thoughts before every game, and she really challenged us to focus on something and then afterward she really brought us all together. I think that left a huge impact on my life. She had this incredible gift for bringing people together, and she ultimately gave us love and appreciation. We all knew it and we all felt it. We all treated each other with that same respect because she demanded it, and there was definitely mutual respect. I've always tried to emulate that because she was an incredible person.

Table 4.5 presents themes generated for question 5 through the utilization of NVivo qualitative analysis software.

Table 4.5

Question 5 Discovered Themes, Word Count, and Weighted Percentages

Themes	Word Count
Weighted Percentage	
1. Kind	15
.17%	
2. Needed	13
.64%	
3. People	13
.64%	
4. Respect	12
.60%	
5. Example	9
.45%	

Question 6.

What additional thoughts would you like to share regarding the role that love plays in servant leadership?

P1 shared the following:

It is a little voice inside of you that tells you the proper things to do in your life, even the hard things. It's that voice that Heavenly Father instills in you that everyone is born with. I have had a lot of different experiences, and I think I have learned from them. I am totally amazed at the difference between a person who cares, and someone who operated completely the opposite of that, who is selfish, and can be very mean at times. It is just the way to be.

P5 shared the following:

I don't think you have servant leadership if you don't have love. A lot of people haven't learned how to love. There's a man that lives in our community that I saw the other day, and he grew up with one foot in the drug culture and one out, but I heard him say one time that you have to get to the point in life where you love someone else more than you love yourself. There are a lot of people that get there; we do love ourselves which is not wrong but very few reach a point where they love someone else more, or others more than they love themselves. Certain leadership requires a tremendous amount of self-sacrifice, and that's hard. It's okay to do it in an episodic way, particularly if the cameras are rolling but it's harder to do it constantly, when no one is noticing. It's a rare quality, it can be found, and it can be developed; there's no bounds to the impact that it can have.

P10 shared the following:

Let me say one other thing, that I meant to say at the very first. To be a good leader, you have to believe what your product or your service is. We have to believe that we are going to give a great experience, that it's going to be worth their money. Whatever our mission is, we have to believe in it. Most leaders that I know, that are great leaders of great companies, they believe in their product. I love Apple products, they are ridiculously expensive, but they are so cool and when Steve Jobs started his company, though I may have disagreed with his politics, he was happy, and his company beamed with "We are what is happening, we are cool, we are happy." I think most successful companies, more or less, may not specifically talk about love but it's very positive, a very positive message, a very confident message. I think that therefore that inner love has a huge impact but not in a very overt way usually. It comes out in things like my employees in trouble, what do I do? Or here's a charity that really needs our help, but most of the time, it's unseen and unheard.

Table 4.6 presents themes for question 6 generated through the utilization of NVivo qualitative analysis software.

Table 4.6

Question 6 Discovered Themes, Word Count, and Weighted Percentages

Themes	Word Count
Weighted Percentage	
1. People	36
3.1%	
2. World	10
.86%	
3. Better	8
.69%	
4. Feeling	8
.69%	
5. Selfishness	8
.69%	

P7 shared the following:

You can't be a servant leader without having genuine love, and if you don't genuinely love yourself, you can't genuinely love others, you can't purely love others. I'm not perfect at it. We all have faults but that's what's great about life. We are here to try to become better, and I feel a great desire and responsibility to inspire my team to want to become better in all areas of their lives, and more importantly, their personal lives, their lives with a higher Being. I believe in God, and in Jesus Christ, but not all people do, but I believe that it's important for me when I get up in the morning to help others realize how truly good they are. If you don't lead by serving, if you don't lead with respect and with kindness, then how are you leading? You're leading by dictatorship, or by demands, and that just creates a miserable work environment for people. Now I understand that some people need a little more direction, or potentially a little more hand holding, that's typically not my style of leadership, but you can still do that with love even if that's what's needed or necessary. I think that love is the critical element, it is the most important aspect of servant leadership.

P6 shared the following:

When I talk about sponsoring the next generation, preparing the next generation, part of that is selfishly driven, you know, I don't want to work forty or fifty hours a week for the rest of my life. I mean I love it, but I also want more freedom and flexibility, so we are trying to replace me. I find that it is harder for younger men, I am not sure if women have the same problem, in general, to have the same patience, and love the people with whom they work or have stewardship over. I have been giving him more and more responsibility, he is better at the business in every single way than I am, except that one area. We talk about it very openly and candidly, I say look, you have to treat your employees like customers. You can't be harsh, you can't be demanding. He is not about ninety-nine percent of the time, but every once in a while, he wants to get it done, and he is direct. That directness can be perceived as sometimes being something other than direct. Some people may be gifted to naturally be that way, but I want to know how to instill in him these qualities at a younger age. How do you train someone else if they are not naturally driven that way? I can kind of see myself at that age, I mean, things were more black-and-white. It is not always about who is right, it is about what is right.

Table 4.7 presents themes generated when analyzing all the interview questions as one set of data, through the utilization of NVivo qualitative analysis software.

Table 4.7

All Questions Discovered Themes, Word Count, and Weighted Percentages

Themes	Word Count
Weighted Percentage	
1. People	155
1.85%	
2. Feeling	73
.87%	
3. Needs	50
.60%	
4. Caring	47
.56%	
5. Giving	44
.53%	

Summary

After a thematic analysis of the interview data, it was found that the themes for the role of love in servant leadership are the following: people, caring, serve, feeling, and relationships. The themes found for the significance of love in today's leadership culture are the following: people, feeling, different, better, and world.

Chapter 4 presented the data gathered in a non-evaluative manner. Chapter 5 will present the data using an evaluative approach, summarize the findings, present the conclusion from the research, review the implications of the study, and present opportunities for future research.

Chapter 5:

Summary, Conclusions, and Recommendations

Introduction

Chapter 5 contains a comprehensive summary of the study, presents a summary of findings and conclusions, reviews the theoretical implications of the study, reviews practical implications of the study, presents recommendations for future research, presents recommendations for practice, and will finish with concluding remarks.

Summary of the Study

The goal of this study was to open future research and discussion that will revolutionize a paradigm shift in the way business leaders approach leadership. The paradigm shift that I am speaking of is a shift from seeing business leadership through the lens of power and authority, to seeing leadership as a means for serving and lifting all within the business organization.

Summary of Findings and Conclusion

What is the role of love in servant leadership?

People. The number one theme found throughout this study, and

specifically regarding the role of love in servant leadership, is *people*. Servant leaders show love through being people focused. Tanno conducted a phenomenological study, in which he interviewed high-level executive servant leaders and found that servant leaders saw themselves as stewards over the people that directly report to them (Tanno, 2017). Servant leaders place a high level of importance on meeting the needs of their people. This people focus is not just directed to the employees; it is directed to customers, vendors, and every stakeholder in the business. Each one of these relationships is valuable to the servant leader, and being people focused helps keep these critical business relationships strong. P8 shared the following regarding the importance of people:

I wholeheartedly believe that this is where the right kind of leadership lies, in truly and genuinely loving people. After doing this with employees, the most important thing that I have discovered is that it's about the people. It's about connecting people, it's part of my mission statement. I'm trying to connect people one cookie at a time. It's the people that come into the shop that I get to meet and hear their stories, it's the people that are coming and asking questions about why I did this, what the story is, and it's also about connecting a group of people who otherwise wouldn't be friends. They are coming together as a team and working toward the same goal. For me, it's about the people one hundred percent, and I probably overpay my people but it's because I appreciate them, and I know that ultimately they will reciprocate. They work hard, and they are amazing. I have a great group of girls who work tirelessly. They have a purpose and as I express my love for the people and the experiences that we share. I think that they feel the same way. They love seeing the people come in and their experience and happiness. It's all about the people and the experiences that we can share together. I love it. Just trying to help people understand that it's more than just cookies; it's about people connecting, and sometimes that happens by eating a cookie. I feel like it's a great experience for people to see something that's not just coming to a job and getting a paycheck. It's about what experiences you can have that day with people that come in and with the people that you work with.

Caring. This study found *caring* to be a theme that emerged from the interview data. Greenleaf asserted that servant leaders serve the needs of the employees and customers first to create a more caring and just society (Greenleaf, 1977). Servant leaders may not use the term *love* with their employees, but they show love to their employees through their caring actions. For many servant leaders, love is the motivating force behind how they approach and handle every business situation that arises. When this happens, a caring work environment can emerge where the employee feels like an important member of a work family. Nishii (2017) found that servant leaders were caring, kind, and nice, but that they showed that they cared through tough love, leap-ahead care, and empowerment. Having a servant leader care for employees in a genuine manner is a way that love is shown to employees and all stakeholders. P1 shared the following regarding what love is:

> Love is caring. If you do not love somebody, how can you care about them? They are human beings. I would say maybe that I am a little different than some people, having gone through the Vietnam War when I was a very young man of 17 and 18. I have been to other places, I have seen extreme things, and it has made me who I am today. I do care about others, and I have a lifetime of action to show that. It makes you feel good; that is what we are supposed to do. Our Heavenly Father cares about us, he has taught us to care about others, and it works.

Serve. This study found *serve* to be a theme that emerged from the interview data. Servant leaders serve their employees, customers, suppliers, and other stakeholders. When you love someone, you are willing to serve them. Serving those whom the leader has stewardship over is a core concept of servant leadership and is one way that leaders show their love. Tanno conducted a qualitative study with high-level executive servant leaders and found that servant leaders do not limit their service to direct reports. Tanno found that servant leaders serve all the stakeholders of the business (Tanno, 2017).

Instilling a service culture is a way for all members of the organization to show love one to another, increase morale, and increase customer service. When employees are served by their leaders, they feel loved and appreciated. When the needs of the employees are served, it can set in motion a greater desire for the employees to serve the customers. It is critical for servant leaders to serve frontline associates, because the frontline associates are the face of the business—they need to be happy employees, they bring in the money, and they interact face to face with customers. Served employees can translate into served repeat customers. Some leaders view serving others as being weak (Johnson, 2009). Servant leaders need to be unapologetic in their service of others and need to demonstrate a mental toughness to overcome this perception. P4 shared the following regarding how the greatest leaders are best servants:

Again, because of my background, the greatest leaders in a biblical sense, in a scriptural sense, are the best servants, in that they are willing to do whatever it takes to help the people they are serving and interacting with. As they act as a servant, it shows the people whom they are serving that this person cares and, again, are much more likely to accept any insights, help, correction, or knowledge that might be given, and because that person has come to realize that this person isn't just leading over him or her, but they lead by example, and they serve to enhance their leadership.

Feeling. This study found *feeling* to be one of the themes that

emerged from the interview data. Servant leaders show love for their employees by paying attention to how employees are feeling. Jit, Sharma, and Kawatra found in a qualitative study that servant leaders contribute to an emotionally healing work environment (Jit, Sharma, & Kawatra, 2017). Creating an emotionally healing environment is one way in which servant leaders show love to employees and associates. It is important for servant leaders to have a workforce that is feeling energized, happy, productive, and appreciated. Leadership is more than making sure a job gets done; it is making sure a job gets done, while at the same time making sure that your team is emotionally healthy. Servant leaders have the unique ability to have high-performing teams, while at the same time having the emotional intelligence to ensure individuals on the team are feeling great. P8 shared how important it is for employees to feel loved, accepted, and appreciated:

You can feel love and you can see love, it's something that is very present, and I see so many people running away from that because of selfish reasons or feeling that they are not accepted and running away from something, whatever that might be. I think that if people knew that they were loved or felt accepted, in the end they would act differently. That can go to any culture, whether that is our culture presently or any time in history, if people feel a genuine love they are going to act differently, and they will reciprocate. I met with a CEO of a huge company and he mentioned that the turnover rate was 400 percent, and that to me just means that there was no gathering or feeling of love or appreciation. People will walk away if they don't feel that love. Sometimes it's not even about the money; it's just about feeling like you are part of a team and feeling accepted. That was interesting to me, because I do things that are out of the ordinary but it's because I believe in people. If that says anything, I think that's huge, it means people will really help run a business, no matter how great your leadership skills are.

Relationships. This study found *relationships* to be one of the themes that emerged from the interview data. Servant leaders place a very high priority on making and keeping healthy relationships with employees, associates, customers, suppliers, and other business connections. Chung conducted a study that explored servant leadership traits from the life of Jesus, and found team building and relationships as themes in the data (Chung, 2011). Because of the love and respect that servant leaders have for others, they can have very good relationships. Servant leaders do not see employees, customers, or vendors as a nuisance; they see them as critical relationships that are needed to maintain business success. P2 shared the following regarding the effects that establishing loving relationships could have:

> If there were greater love in leadership roles, such as in boss-employee roles, and business-customer relationships, I think that this segment of society, if you will, the business world would be a better place. The world would be a better place if there were a greater love in the business segment of society. This is where our society is falling apart. I have lived in different parts of the world, and in the world and in this country, there is so much divisiveness, and everybody seems to care about their opinion, and themselves, to the exclusion of everyone else. It is divisive, it is destructive, and it tears apart the moral fabric of society. I think that many of the ills that we see in this country is a result of breakdown in true love for one's fellow being here on earth.

What do you think is the significance of love in today's leadership culture?

People. The number one theme found throughout this study, and

specifically regarding the significance of love in today's leadership

culture, is *people*. This study found that today's leadership culture

needs to improve regarding how leaders treat the people of the

businesses they serve. This study found that love is often a missing

component in today's leadership culture. P5 shared how loving and

serving the people of the business is something that we have lost

touch with:

> I don't think that it is significant. I think only in the
>
> most tertiary way. It is something that we tend to give lip
>
> service to, it is the way we say goodbye on the phone. It has
>
> almost no meaning, so when you try to define love as a type
>
> of love defined by the Greeks as godlike, we do not know
>
> what that is I don't think. We have pretty well lost touch with
>
> that in a lot of regards. It would be significant, but I just do
>
> not see it much. You see it in a few people who are willing to
>
> certainly do things without the recognition and do them

constantly over an extended period of time, and those people had a great impact on my life. For me, they have been remarkable leaders, but I do not know if in any context, would they be anointed or proclaimed as leaders in a worldly sense, because much of what they did was unknown and only known by those who were the beneficiaries. It is so contrary to who we are.

Feeling. This study found *feeling* to be one of the themes that

emerged from the interview data. Leaders need to have more than a high IQ when it comes to leadership. Leaders need to possess emotional intelligence in order to thrive as a business leader. Learning business management topics, such as spreadsheets, balance sheets, cash flow, and net income, are critical to managing a business. However, business is essentially a network of business relationship, and business managers need to have a skill set that includes being a leader who feels and perceives the emotions of others and effectively manages them. There is no stopping a business leader who knows the technical side of the business and can effectively keep business relationships healthy. Jit, Sharma, and

Kawatra argued that because servant leaders are more apt to serve than non servant leaders, they are better able to care for the emotional needs of employees (Jit, Sharma, & Kawatra, 2017). Business leaders of the 21st century need to have a skill set that balances the operational side of the business with the development of current employees. P5 shared the following regarding the importance of treating employees well:

> Because we are a small company, I look at it as an employer-employee relationship. We don't have huge departments so everyone in the business gets to wear multiple hats, which gives them a chance to grow and experience more and not be bored hopefully. One of the things that I think that's important as I read books and talk to other business leaders and such is that these employees, I don't think of them as employees, when you're speaking about that relationship, at times you have to define it like that for people to understand the relationship but when I'm speaking about them in their presence I use the term associate or partner. I think it's important that you see them as human beings not a tool of the business, they are, but what I've

learned is to treat them as a peer, don't ever forget they are a human being, that has feelings, has needs, wants to succeed. Everybody wants to be needed, everybody wants to feel important, everybody wants to feel like they're contributing,

Different. This study found *different* to be one of the

themes that emerged from the interview data. There are two ways you can approach leadership. First, you could approach it from a position of power and authority, or you can approach it from a position of love. Power and authority will work for the short-term, however over the long-term it can have a devastating effect on the company culture, employee morale, employee turnover, training costs, etc. Ebener, and O'Connell stated that servant leaders are more likely to serve than be served, more likely to recognize than be recognized, and more likely to extend power than exercise power over others (Ebener & O'Connell, 2010). The researcher asserts that leading with love makes a positive difference. Also, leaders who lead with power and authority need to choose a different approach to leadership. There is a different way than leading with fear. It is possible to learn how to lead with love. P1 shared the following regarding the two ways of leading:

Well, I guess there are two ways to do it. You can do it by threats, by a position of power, or you can be a nice guy, and try and work things out. You need people to do things for you in business, and in other roles in your life like church and politics. Having been on the city council also, working with others is the first thing that I decided was important. It's not always my way, you can learn from other people. If you jump right in there and tell them how it's going to be, a lot of times it is not going to work out that way. You are better off to not be so forceful, hear everybody's opinion, and maybe take the middle ground. That is working with people.

Better. This study found *better* to be one of the themes that emerged from the interview data. Servant leaders know that there is a better way to lead that can result in better business results. Leading from a foundation of love is the better way, and a happier more productive workforce is the better result. When love is the motivator in business leadership, care is taken to make sure that each situation is handled in the most appropriate way. Servant leaders can give corrective feedback to employees in a way that inspires change and increases productivity.

Servant leaders want to develop the talents of their employees and help them become better in every aspect of their life. Continuous betterment of self and others is a daily pursuit. Utilizing love is the better way to lead, and it results in better business results, and can ultimately facilitate the betterment of society. P9 shared the following regarding how giving corrective feedback to employees is a form of love, because it is making the employee a better person and employee:

There are probably times that my employees might not feel loved. In those moments where I have to take them aside privately and reprimand them or tell them that they are doing something wrong, they may not necessarily think I'm being loving. But I'm a strong believer, especially with my teaching background, that helping. I do have adult employees, but with my teenage employees, most of them, this is their first job. I think of it as it's my job in teaching them and molding them how to have a job, how to be a good employee. So, I will reprimand them when needed, I will tell them when they are doing something wrong. In those moments they may not feel like I'm showing them love but, it really is because I'm helping them become better human beings, better people. I'm a pretty loving person. I can still love someone even when they are being difficult, it takes a lot for me to not love someone. It's just in my nature, just who I am.

World. This study found *world* to be one of the themes that emerged from the interview data. The business world would be a better place, and the world would be a better place if we approached each business transaction, and each business dealing from a position of love. This study found that there is a lack of love in leadership in the business world. Leadership is more than receiving a business degree and having management experience. There is a human aspect of management and leadership that cannot be overlooked. Otherwise, a manager who shows a lack of love in his or her leadership style can result in a trail of broken business relationships. Lack of love in leadership can lead to a decrease in employee morale, employee productivity, and employee organizational commitment.

Business leaders, and other leaders throughout the world, seem to have their hearts failing them. The researcher asserts that approaching leadership from a position of love is the right thing to do, and it can result in an approach that helps increase employee morale, employee productivity, and organizational commitment. Increasing love in leadership could have effects that spill over into the overall economy and could end up transforming the world for the better. Chang and Mansford conducted a comparative study of agape love and Confucian Ren and concluded that agape love and Confucian Ren can both be used to help create a more ecumenical world (Chang & Mansford, 2016). Love applied in leadership is a concept that could improve the business world, in a dramatic, and positive way. P7 shared the following regarding what could happen if there were greater love throughout the world:

It's huge, because I look at the world at large, and if we just had more love for each other, I think the world would be in a much better place. I think we are too busy today about power, about prestige, about money, and different things drive the world, and drive different people. If people could go about every day with love being their guide, I think the world would be a completely different place. Not just the world at large, but the business world so to speak.

I think if we could identify that we are all brothers and sisters, no matter what race, no matter what religion, no matter what culture, no matter what ethnicity we might be, if we could look at whoever it is across from us, ultimately you are my brother or sister. Therefore, I'm going to treat you with love and respect because of that reason only, that singular reason. I think the significance of it is huge because I think we would see a huge shift that would be one of peace and hope. I know that might sound trite, but it would be better if we could remember where we came from, who we came from, and who we are a part of. If we could just start from a place of love, it would just be a huge paradigm shift.

Implications

Theoretical implications. Servant leadership must have the ability to balance the operational needs of the business with the development of employees. It can be compared to an airplane: One wing of the airplane represents the operational side of the organization; the other wing represents the development of the employees' side of the organization. The servant leader can be compared to the pilot of the plane. The pilot needs to be properly trained on how to keep the plane stable, in order to nimbly navigate the plane around dangerous storms, find new destinations, and find the most effective routes.

An effective servant leader does not focus just on the operational side of the organization, nor does the servant leader focus just on developing employees within an organization. When the operations of the business are focused on too heavily, the people of the organization begin to suffer. When the development of employees is focused on too heavily, then the operations of the organization begin to suffer. This imbalance of focus makes it impossible for the servant leader to stabilize the plane. Servant leadership theory is the ability to balance the operations of the business with the development of employees. Servant leaders balance both wings of the airplane, so that the airplane can achieve forward and upward momentum. The successful servant leader can take the airplane to new heights and steer it toward new destinations if the operations of the business and the development of employees are properly balanced. With proper leadership training, the servant leader can take control of the plane and fly employees and organizations successfully through the business gauntlet of the 21st century in a way that only a servant leader can do.

Practical implications. There are two sides regarding the role that love plays in servant leadership, and both sides are a form of showing love. The one side is loving employees, and the other side involves giving improvement feedback when needed. Love involves cheerleading, serving, caring for, supporting, providing resources, etc. Improvement feedback means properly and promptly coaching the employees on how to become their best. Servant leaders show love to their employees by helping them become the best that they can be in their work environment. This involves striking the proper balance of encouragement and improvement feedback. feedback.

Servant leaders can be viewed by authoritative leaders as being weak, and unable to provide proper improvement feedback. This perception can lead to the servant leaders being passed up for promotions (Riordan, 2010). It is important for servant leaders to develop their own skills regarding providing improvement feedback. The researcher found that servant leaders can be effective leaders when they are able provide both love, and corrective feedback when needed. Employees may not know how to become their best, if their servant leader is too afraid to tell them what needs to improve. There is no need for a servant leader to be fearful of giving improvement feedback. The reason why is because a servant leader approaches corrective feedback from a standpoint of love and can present the feedback in a way that builds capability. The servant leader is honest with employees and seeks honesty from others as to how he or she can improve. Servant leadership is loving employees, and this means taking the tough road by showing love and by being honest with employees about expectations and improvement.

Recommendations for future research

This research opens the door for more research opportunities within the topic of love and servant leadership. The first recommendation for future research would be to duplicate the same research study in a new geographical location. All the participants from this study ended up being found in Wasatch County and Utah County within the State of Utah, within the United States of America. It would be beneficial to duplicate the study in various cultures around the world, where business and cultural norms may differ.

The second recommendation for future research would be to duplicate the study focusing on a certain sector of the economy, such as the primary sector, the manufacturing sector, the service sector, or the academic sector. This study did not have a focus on a sector of the economy, and it would be beneficial to narrow the focus of the study to one major sector of the economy.

The third recommendation for future research is to duplicate the study within the nonprofit sector exclusively. This study did not specify whether a participant needed to be from a for-profit or nonprofit industry. This study only had one participant who came from a nonprofit organization. It would be beneficial to discover the role that love plays in servant leadership from leaders exclusively within nonprofit organizations.

The fourth recommendation for future research is to duplicate the study and compare the differences between for-profit servant leaders and nonprofit servant leaders regarding the role that love plays in servant leadership. This study had one participant from the nonprofit sector and nine participants from the for-profit sector. It would be interesting to explore if there is a difference between how each group views the role of love in servant leadership.

The fifth recommendation for future research is to extend the research into one of the other attributes of a servant leader as discovered by Focht and Ponton. This study focused on the role of love in servant leadership, but a deeper study of the role of any of the attributes of servanthood would be of value. The twelve values that Focht and Ponton found in a Delphi study are the following: valuing people, humble, listening, trusting, caring, having integrity, serving, empowering, serving others' needs before their own, collaborating, loving unconditionally, and learning (Focht & Ponton, 2015).

The sixth recommendation for future research, which is the next step for this research, is to explore how servant leaders instill love in their managers. I had multiple participants express a desire to know how to instill love in the managers or executives of their organizations. These individuals seemed to have all the technical skills of the business but lacked when it came to showing love and appreciation to direct reports. Exploring how to instill love in leaders would be beneficial to the business leadership community.

Recommendations for practice

Treat employees as customers. Several of the participants mentioned the importance of treating employees as customers of the business. This was a concept that was not specifically found in the literature review, even though the concept fits well within the servant leadership framework. There are a lot of parallels between the importance of happy customers and the importance of happy employees. Both are vital to the success of the business because without one or the other, the business, more than likely, does not exist. The mistreatment of employees can lead to the employees mistreating customers. On the flip side, if employees are treated well, it can result in employees treating customers well. Treatment can flow downstream in organizations. For this reason, I believe it is critical to treat employees as assets of the organization that will give us their repeat business of continuing to work for the organization in an effective way.

Businesses want to satisfy customer needs in such a way that they become repeat customers, talk favorably about the organization on social media, bring friends to the business, etc. Providing exceptional customer service is key strategy to attracting and retaining a strong customer base. The same can be said about the employer-employee relationship. You could say that employees are, in effect, volunteers of the business, and are free to leave at any time. They too give ratings on employment sites and share feelings on social media. It is critical that leaders are able see employees as key players of the organization that need to be acquired and retained, just as the customers need to be acquired and retained.

Selfishness: The lack of love. Selfishness was

mentioned by many participants as a key factor that underpins why businesses fail, why businesses can have a bad image, why leaders fail to show love to their employees, and as a root cause of the decay of the moral fabric of society. If selfishness can cause the aforementioned harm, then selflessness could be seen as the antidote to increasing business success rates, improving the image of business, increasing the love shown to employees, and aiding the healing of the moral fabric of society. Service was found in the study to be a key way that a servant leader shows love for employees. Nishii, when interviewing 15 servant leaders, found that servant leaders often preferred to serve the needs of others in the organization behind the scenes, or quietly when no one was watching. Serving the needs of others was their focus, and they did not want recognition for it (Nishii, 2017). Servant leaders, of course care about themselves, but they do make a concerted effort to be selfless regarding developing employees' capabilities and giving them the tools that they need to succeed. P2 shared the following regarding the root cause of a lack of love:

It is an attitude of selfishness, and I think this attitude of selfishness is creating many of the problems that we see in society today. Some of the trends that are most disturbing in our country with regards to everything from political divisiveness, to the drug society, to children being raised without parents, or without at least one parent in the home roots back into this whole issue of selfishness. I think that until we address the issue of selfishness at its root cause and start somehow to become more caring of other people, and not only ourselves, then I think the trends that are damaging our society will continue. This is just a piece of that, but I think that it is a place that can be addressed.

There is a lot of mistrust of business in the world because there have been a lot of people who have been abused or hurt by business in one form or another, financial or otherwise. People sell services or products that are not what they are represented to be, and it hurts people. It is a result of selfishness, it is a result of caring about my bottom line as opposed to what I am doing to the individuals that I am supposedly serving. The problem of a lack of love is one symptom of a larger problem that exists in the world today, and that is the selfish nature that seems to be getting worse over time.

P2 also stated the following:

I am trying to relate this to a previous boss of mine back east who was a very successful financial advisor and I worked for him. He eventually turned into somebody who became unethical at best, and illegal practices at worst. His business at one point was the largest privately held wealth management practices in America. His greediness combined with his unethical practices ended up destroying the company completely. Clients of his felt like he had taken advantage of them, and lawsuits came as a result. Again, it was this lack of concern for his clients that destroyed his business. If he had a concern for the client as much as he did for his own wealth, he wouldn't have done those things he did that were unethical. Because he had lost the trust of his clientele, he went out of business. He had a very profitable and very successful company but because he cared about his own pocket, it eventually caught up to him and destroyed his company.

Servant leadership: Not a passive activity. It was

found in the study that servant leaders showing love is not a passive

activity and is usually not the easy road for the leader to take. Tanno

found in a study that servant leaders served customers, employees,

the organization, and stakeholders (Tanno, 2017). Serving the needs

of so many can be a daunting challenge and requires perseverance.

Harper found in a qualitative study that perseverance was an

emergent theme from the study of a love-driven leader (Harper,

2017). This study found that showing love is tenaciously holding

employees accountable. One of the criticisms of servant leadership is

that servant leaders lack ability to assert authority over others

(Johnson, 2001). The researcher found that servant leaders can

tenaciously hold others accountable in a way that motivates and

inspires. Love is having the honesty to tell an employee where

improvements can be made, love is strong and immovable, love is

pushing employees to be the very best that they can be, love is

rewarding extra results with extra compensation, love is letting an

employee go who is not a good fit for the organization, love is

getting out of the office and working side by side with direct reports, love is taking care of the stakeholders of an organization, and love

can be shown through protecting others when needed. P5 shared the

following story of a servant leader who was relentless:

This is a question where I kind of feel at home with

your topic. This was an individual I had met as a young

missionary. He had grown up in a non-religious background,

and as I recall, he was from Missouri. He was a tough guy.

His father used to discipline him. Whenever they would have

some kind of difficulty, his father would take him out to a

boxing ring that he had put up in the shed, he would put on

his gloves with his father, and they would go at it. That was

the way that he was raised. He was a big man physically. He

joined The Church of Jesus Christ of Latter-day Saints

through his wife who quietly was just faithful. He literally

threw several sets of missionaries out of his house physically.

Only one of them came back. He was an interesting man,

even today, fifty years later, I don't think I have ever met

anyone quite like him in terms of leadership. He was really

tough. He would push you to the point where you would

almost break, but you kind of knew that he would fight for

you and would do so physically if need be. A couple of missionaries got roughed up by a man, and he found out about it. He went over to see the guy despite the missionary's protests. He approached the man's home and knocked on the door. The man came to the screen door, and he looked at him, and said are you coming out or am I coming in? And that was kind of his way of saying hello, and he physically threatened the guy. He said if you ever do this again, this and that will happen. You kind of knew, in a really organic way that he would take care of us, so we would do anything for him.

He and I were released from our missions about the same time, he was a young man even then, much younger than I am now. He had cancer, and it was terminal. I remember seeing him shortly before he passed away. I introduced my fiancée to him, who is now my wife. I asked him how he was, and he said I'm fine. I said I understand that, but how are you? He said, I have never known the emotion of fear in all my life, and I am not afraid now. He said I think the Lord has just offered me a transfer, and I have decided to accept it. He went through death just like he went through life, he just had no fear of anything. I think that I found myself completely changed in terms of how I saw love, and how I saw love interacting with other people. I learned that sometimes you love other people by slamming them up against a wall, sometimes literally. And I saw him with lots of young men. One had gotten out of prison before he had become a missionary, I didn't know that was what happened. But I watched this man drive all night to find him one night. This missionary had gotten himself lost, he found him, rehabilitated him, and made him into a great missionary. He kind of did that over, and over again, with everybody, irrespective of what their background was. He would always say, "come on, you have got to be strong, you have got to be strong." I suppose there aren't many days that I haven't thought about him. He had a really powerful imprinting on my life. If I were to point to one person, and he was a leader, I mean everyone, in a business sense, in whatever circle he was, he was the leader, I mean he just looked it. So, I saw early on, what you are talking about, but I have seldom seen it since. At least in that kind of magnitude. I didn't ever really see him do anything because he wanted someone else to see him doing it, he just did it. Sometimes it wasn't very conventional, a lot of times it wasn't conventional, but that didn't seem to bother him either. But, over and over again I saw him demonstrate what you are talking about here. So, if there is any degree that I have tried to adopt what you are talking about, it would be because of him, as I saw that in him. He was a convert to the Church when he was 27 years old. He was the top beer salesman in the United States. He joined the Church and had to quit his job. The next year and a half, all that he could find to do was to sweep out a warehouse at night. He was kind of okay with this, he had decided this was right and he went forward with it and that's kind of the way he was. If it was right, he could do it, and we'd follow him, we'd follow him anywhere. He died very young, but he had a dramatic impact on my life in terms of what you're talking about.

A better way to do business. It was found in the

study, that there needs to be much more love infused into the

leadership culture of business; that if leaders would utilize love in

their business interactions and transactions, the world would be a

much better place to do business. The trust within the business

community would increase, and the cost to do business would go

down, resulting in an overall increase in revenue for the business

community. P4 shared the following regarding what happens when

we approach leadership with love:

> Not to sound sappy, but to quote the Beatles, "All you
>
> need is love," which I just did, but I believe it's true. It's
>
> absolutely crucial that people have a genuine love if they
>
> expect to have people respond to them in a positive way.
>
> Disagreements absolutely occur, but if there is an underlying
>
> love for the people that we serve, not only is it in most cases
>
> returned to that leader, there's a feeling of love that radiates
>
> back from the person that's getting instruction. But it just
>
> seems to cause the whole situation in a business, in a
>
> classroom, in life, in marriages and families, if we do things

motivated by a love for, let's say God, and he would then have us love our fellowmen, that just seems to breed an atmosphere of charity, and cooperation, and there's no question that that works.

Paul in his writings to the Corinthians gives the bold assertion that love never fails (1 Cor. 13:8, The New King James Version), and later counsels that all things be done in love (1 Cor. 16:14, The New King James Version). The infusion of love in servant leadership is a leadership concept that has the potential for changing the business world for the better and has the possibility to change the world.

The researcher found that the command-and-control style of leadership is a leadership style that does not produce lasting results. There are short-term results with the command-and-control method, but the results will have diminishing returns over time, and employees will, in the end, choose to leave the organization. The researcher found that there are leaders who can have all the knowledge in the world, but if they do not possess love in their leadership style, they can be a very destructive leader. The following is a dramatic experience that P1 shared from the Vietnam War that demonstrates the difference between a leader who cared and a leader who only cared about himself:

I had a First Sergeant in Vietnam who was a great guy. We all loved him. He cared about us; we knew he did. He showed us that by how he would talk to us, and the things that he would tell us that we were going to do. He would explain things, and we knew that he was not going to get us all killed. I was in an airborne infantry outfit, and we knew that when we were under his direction that we would be OK. He ended up getting shot up and getting sent back to the States, and he was replaced by another Sergeant Major that was completely opposite of this guy. He was out for himself; he was out to make himself a hero, and was totally different. He did not care about the guys, he treated them bad, he was getting people killed. I had a friend who was only an E3 who got in this Sergeant Major's face and told him what he thought of him. Of course, the Sergeant Major did not like that, so he did not like my friend. The villages were off limit to us at the time, so the only place you could go off the base was to a garbage dump. The Sergeant Major came and got me one day and told me to bring my weapon and come with him. He took me to the garbage dump, and I could not believe it, my friend was standing sixty or seventy feet away. He ordered me to shoot my friend. It totally blew me away. I have no idea why he thought that I would do this. I turned around and loaded my M-16, I turned it on full auto, and I was going to turn around and shoot the Sergeant Major. I turned around and a loud voice said to me three times, do not shoot this man. I ignored the voice the first two times and was just going to shoot him, but the third time I got the message. I turned back around, dropped the clip out, jacked the round out of the chamber, and I threw the M-16 at the Sergeant Major. He locked me up in a Conex container for five days and busted me down to private. He dropped me four grades and wrote in the paperwork that I had gone crazy and left the base without permission. So that is a very stark contrast between someone who cared and someone who only cared about himself. I know that is a pretty extreme story, but I have lots of those.

Concluding Remarks

This paper is the start of a better way to do business, a better way to lead employees, a better way to increase revenue, a better way to compete in the marketplace, a better way to increase employee productivity, and a better way to lead organizations through the twenty-first century. This study has shown how critically important it is for servant leaders, and all leaders alike, to cultivate and utilize love in leadership practices. The role that love has in servant leadership is a role that cannot be understated. Love is the underpinnings of the servant leadership framework. Servant leadership is a leadership model that can be applied by business leaders of all faiths. A business leader does not need to be Christian to effectively utilize servant leadership. Treating others as you would like to be treated is a concept that transcends religious lines and brings the human family onto common ground.

Love in servant leadership means being people centered. Love in servant leadership means being caring. Love in servant leadership means serving others. It means having emotional intelligence. Love in servant leadership means developing relationships. Love in servant leadership is a different but right approach to leadership. Love in servant leadership makes people, and businesses better. Love in servant leadership could change the business world, and in turn change the world. What is the role of love in servant leadership? Without love there is no servant leadership.

References

Awan, K. Z., Qureshi, I., & Arif, S. (2012). The effective leadership style in NGOs: Impact of servant leadership style on employees' work performance and mediation effect of work motivation. *International Journal of Economics and Management Sciences, 1*(11), 43–56.

Barbuto, J. E., Jr., & Wheeler, D. W. (2006). Scale development and construct clarification of servant leadership. *Group & Organization Management, 31*, 300–326. doi:10.1177/1059601106287091

Borchers, K. (2016). *Servant leadership and job satisfaction in a Christian faith-based nonprofit older adult healthcare organization* (Doctoral dissertation). Available from ProQuest Dissertations & Theses Global. (Order No. 10137839)

Burden, A. K. (2014). *Servant leadership and job satisfaction* (Doctoral dissertation). (Order No. 3634201). Available from ProQuest Dissertations & Theses Global: The Humanities and Social Sciences Collection. Retrieved from https://search-proquest-com.libraryresources.columbiasouthern.edu/docview/1612628928?accountid=33337. (1612628928)

Cox, L., Graves, D., & McCann, J. T. (2014). Servant leadership, employee satisfaction, and organizational performance in rural community hospitals. *International Journal of Business and Management, 9*(10). doi:10.5539/ijbm.v9n10p28

Chang, W., & Mansford Prior, J. (2016). Confucian ren and Jesus' agape as a basic virtue toward a more ecumenical world. *Journal of Ecumenical Studies, 51*, 552–566.

Chung, Y. S. (2011). Why servant leadership? Its uniqueness and principles in the life of Jesus. *Journal of Asia Adventist Seminary, 14*(2), 159–170.

Coetzer, M. F., Bussin, M., & Geldenhuys, M. (2017). The functions of a servant leader. *Administrative Sciences, 7*(1), 1–32. doi:10.3390/admsci7010005

Creswell, J. W. (2014). *Research design: Qualitative, quantitative, and mixed methods approaches* (4th ed.). Thousand Oaks, CA: Sage.

Darawsheh, W. (2014). Reflexivity in research: Promoting rigour, reliability and validity in qualitative research. *International Journal of Therapy & Rehabilitation, 21*, 560–568.

Davenport, B. (2015). Compassion, suffering and servant leadership: Combining compassion and servant leadership to respond to suffering. *Leadership, 11*, 300–315.

Davis, C. J. (2014). *Self-transcendence and servant leadership behavior in new thought spiritual centers: A correlational study* (Doctoral dissertation or master's thesis). (Order No. 3691408). Available from ProQuest Dissertations & Theses Global: The Humanities and Social Sciences Collection. Retrieved from https://search-proquest-com.libraryresources.columbiasouthern.edu/docview/1668318535?accountid=33337. (1668318535)

Dickson, L. R. B. (2008). *A legacy of lifelong learning: Leadership, lessons, love, and laughter in the life of Elizabeth Gammon Pendleton* (Doctoral dissertation or master's thesis). (Order No. 3410179). Available from ProQuest Dissertations & Theses Global: The Humanities and Social Sciences Collection. Retrieved from https://search-proquest-com.libraryresources.columbiasouthern.edu/docview/496950780?accountid=33337. (496950780)

Dierendonck, D., & Patterson, K. (2015). Compassionate love as a cornerstone of servant leadership: An integration of previous theorizing and research. *Journal of Business Ethics, 128*(1), 119–131. doi:10.1007/s10551-014-2085-z

Ebener, D. R., & O'Connell, D. J. (2010). How might servant leadership work? *Nonprofit Management & Leadership, 20,* 315–335.

Ehrhart, M. G. (2004). Leadership and procedural justice climate as antecedents of unit level organizational citizenship behavior. *Journal of Personnel Psychology, 57,* 61–94. doi:10.1111/j.1744-6570-2004.tb02484.x

Faturochman. (1997). The job characteristics theory: A review. *Buletin Psikologi, 2* (December), 1–13.

Focht, A., & Ponton, M. (2015). Identifying primary characteristics of servant leadership: Delphi study. *International Journal of Leadership Studies, 9*(1), 44–61.

Foor, B. (2014). *The role of compassion in servant leadership.* Virginia Beach, VA.: D. Boyer Consulting.

Fried, Y., & Ferris, G. R. (1987). The validity of the job characteristics model: A review and meta-analysis. *Personnel Psychology, 40,* 287–322. doi:10.1111/j.1744-6570. 1987.tb00605.x

George, B. (2003). *Authentic leadership: Rediscovering the secrets to creating lasting value.* San Francisco, CA: Jossey-Bass.

Ginoza, D. Y. (1976). *Christian agape: The basis for an ethical norm and a response to global hunger* (Doctoral dissertation or master's thesis). (Order No. 7619868). Available from ProQuest Dissertations & Theses Global: The Humanities and Social Sciences Collection.

Goodier, B. C., & Eisenberg, E. M. (2006). Seeking the spirit: Communication and the redevelopment of a spiritual organization. *Communication Studies, 57,* 47–66.

Golafshani, N. (2003). Understanding reliability and validity in qualitative research. The *Qualitative Report, 8,* 597–606.

Goleski, G. (2012). *Exploring the way servant leaders foster employee development: A qualitative study of servant leaders in nonprofit organizations.* University of Regina.

Gonwa, J. (2015). Eros, agape, and neighbor-love as ontological gift. *Toronto Journal of Theology, 31*(1), 84–93. doi:10.3138/tjt.3113

Greenleaf, R. K. (1970). *The servant as leader.* Indianapolis, IN: The Robert K. Greenleaf Center.

Greenleaf, R. K. (1972a). *The institution as servant.* Indianapolis, IN: The Robert K. Greenleaf Center.

Greenleaf, R. K. (1972b). *Trustees as servants.* Indianapolis, IN: The Robert K. Greenleaf Center.

Greenleaf, R. K. (2011). *Servant leadership: A journey into the nature of legitimate power and greatness.* New York: Greenleaf Center. (Original work published 1977).

Greenleaf, R. K. (1995). Servant leadership: the leader's companion. *The Free Press*, 20.

Grossi, R. (2016). Which love in law? Zenon Bańkowski and the meaning of love. *Law In Context, 34*(1), 42–57.

Hackman, J., Lawler, E., & Oldham, G. R. (2000). Job characteristics theory. In J. Miner (Ed.), *Organizational behavior: Essential theories of motivation and leadership.* Armonk, NY: M. E.

Hackman, J., & Oldham, G. (1976). Motivation through the design of work: Test of a theory. *Organizational Behavior and Human Performance, 16,* 250–279.

Halter, S. A. (2006). *Agape leadership: Developing selfless love in Christian leadership* (Doctoral dissertation or master's thesis). (Order No. 3214729). Available from ProQuest Dissertations & Theses Global: The Humanities and Social Sciences Collection. Retrieved from https://search-proquest-com.libraryresources.columbiasouthern.edu/docview/304919748?accountid=33337. (304919748)

Hargadon, J. E. (2018). *The effects of servant leadership and job stress on job satisfaction among online university administrators and faculty* (Order No. 10809716). Available from ProQuest Dissertations & Theses Global: The Humanities and Social Sciences Collection. (2038477300).

Harper, D. D. R. (2017). *The love-empowered leader: A qualitative case study of a pastoral leadership exemplar of an evangelical congregation in Virginia* (Doctoral dissertation or master's thesis). (Order No. 10601057). Available from ProQuest Dissertations & Theses Global: The Humanities and Social Sciences Collection. Retrieved from https://search-proquest-com.libraryresources.columbiasouthern.edu/docview/1929519206?accountid=33337. (1929519206)

Harter J., & Adkins A. (2015, April 8). Employees want a lot more from their managers. *Gallup Business Journal.*

Hendrick, C., & Hendrick, S. (1986). A theory and method of love. *Journal of Personality and Social Psychology, 50,* 392–402.

Henning, P. (2016). *The relationship between servant leadership and employee job satisfaction in a colorado nonprofit organization* (Doctoral dissertation or master's thesis). (Order No. 10165397). Available from ProQuest Dissertations & Theses Global: The Humanities and Social Sciences Collection.

Herzberg F. (1968). One more time: How do you motivate employees? *Harvard Business Review, 46*(1), 53–62.

Herzberg F., Mausner, B., & Snyderman, B. (1959). *The motivation to work* (2nd ed.). New York: John Wiley and Sons.

Hodoh, S. D. (2016). *Servant leadership: An effective leadership model for achieving optimal productivity* (Doctoral dissertation or master's thesis). (Order No. 10100517). Available from ProQuest Dissertations & Theses Global: The Humanities and Social Sciences Collection. Retrieved from https://search-proquest-com.libraryresources.columbiasouthern.edu/docview/1784000155?accountid=33337. (1784000155)

Jang, J., & Kandampully, J. (2017): Reducing employee turnover

intention through servant leadership in the restaurant context: A

mediation study of affective organizational commitment.

International Journal of Hospitality & Tourism Administration. doi

10.1080/15256480.2017.1305310

Jit, R., Sharma, C. S., & Kawatra, M. (2017). Healing a broken

spirit: Role of servant leadership. *Vikalpa: The Journal for Decision

Makers, 42*(2), 80–94. doi:10.1177/0256090917703754

Judish, J. E. (1998). Balancing special obligations with the ideal of

agape. *Journal of Religious Ethics, 26*(1), 17.

Johnson, C. E. (2001). *Meeting the ethical challenges of leadership.*

Thousand Oaks, CA: Sage.

Johnson, C. E. (2009). *Meeting the ethical challenges of leadership:

Casting light or shadow.* Thousand Oaks, CA: Sage.

Jordan, M. K. (2015). *Determining the relationship between servant

leadership and job satisfaction among U.S. Navy personnel*

(Doctoral dissertation or master's thesis). (Order No. 3684590).

Available from ProQuest Dissertations & Theses Global: The

Humanities and Social Sciences Collection. Retrieved from

https://libraryresources.columbiasouthern.edu/login?url=https://searc

h-proquest-

com.libraryresources.columbiasouthern.edu/docview/1660746282?a

ccountid=33337. (1660746282)

Kauffman, P. (2013). Eternal love (agape) for the desperate and

poor: The kingdom of God in Paul's Corinth. *International Journal*

of Religion & Spirituality In Society, 3(2), 25–37.

Laub, J. (1999). *Assessing the servant organization: development of*

the servant organizational leadership (SOLA) instrument.

Dissertation Abstracts International, *60*(2), 308. (UMI No. 9921922)

Lewis, R. W., Jr. (1963). *Eros and agape: Ernest Hemingway's love*

ethic (Doctoral dissertation or master's thesis). (Order No. 6406100).

Available from ProQuest Dissertations & Theses Global: The

Humanities and Social Sciences Collection. Retrieved from

https://search-proquest-

com.libraryresources.columbiasouthern.edu/docview/302127364?ac

countid=33337. (302127364)

Liden, R. C., Wayne, S., Zhao. H., & Henderson, D. (2008). Servant

leadership: Development of a multidimensional measure and multi-

level assessment. *Leadership Quarterly, 19*(2), 161.

Linuesa-Langreo, J., Ruiz-Palomino, P., & Elche, D. (2016). Servant leadership, empowerment climate, and group creativity: A case study in the hospitality industry. *Ramon Llull Journal of Applied Ethics*, 7, 9–36.

Lorence, G. J. (2018). *Servant leadership: Its perceived role in predicting effective leadership* (Doctoral dissertation or master's thesis). (Order No. 10687935). Available from ProQuest Dissertations & Theses Global: The Humanities and Social Sciences Collection. Retrieved from https://search-proquest-com.libraryresources.columbiasouthern.edu/docview/1983519835?accountid=33337. (1983519835)

Lub, V. (2015). Validity in qualitative evaluation: Linking purposes, paradigms, and perspectives. *International Journal of Qualitative Methods*, *14*(5), 1–8. doi:10.1177/1609406915621406

Mani, D. (2015). Developmental strategies rooted in the Bible. *Scholedge International Journal of Management & Development*, *2*(4), 25–31.

Martinez, S. (2016). *From novice to expert: The development of a servant leader* (Doctoral dissertation or master's thesis). (Order No. 10143620). Available from ProQuest Dissertations & Theses Global:

The Humanities and Social Sciences Collection. Retrieved from

https://search-proquest-

com.libraryresources.columbiasouthern.edu/docview/1824672439?a

ccountid=33337. (1824672439)

Maslow, A. H. (1943). The theory of human motivation.

Psychological Review, *50*, 370–396. Retrieved from

http://psychclassics.yorku.ca/maslow/motivation.htm

McCann J. T., Graves, D., & Cox. L. (2014). Servant leadership,

employee satisfaction, and organizational performance in rural

community hospitals. *International Journal of Business and*

Management, *9*(10).

Nishii, A. (2017). *Servanthood as love, relationships, and power: A*

heideggerian hermeneutic study on the experiences of servant

leaders (Doctoral dissertation or master's thesis). (Order No.

10601306). Available from ProQuest Dissertations & Theses Global:

The Humanities and Social Sciences Collection. Retrieved from

https://search-proquest-

com.libraryresources.columbiasouthern.edu/docview/1929640947?a

ccountid=33337. (1929640947)

Parris, D. L., Peachey, J. W. (2012). A systematic literature review of servant leadership: Theory in organizational contexts. *Journal of Business Ethics, 113,* 377–393.

Parris, D. L. & Peachey, J. W. (2013). Encouraging servant leadership: A qualitative study of how a cause-related sporting event inspires participants to serve. *Leadership, 9,* 486.

Persaud, D. (2015). *A correlational study of servant leadership and employee job satisfaction in new york city public hospital emergency rooms* (Doctoral dissertation or master's thesis). (Order No. 3689163). Available from ProQuest Dissertations & Theses Global: The Humanities and Social Sciences Collection. Retrieved from https://libraryresources.columbiasouthern.edu/login?url=http://searc h.proquest.com.libraryresources.columbiasouthern.edu/docview/167 8948625?accountid=33337. (1678948625)

Preiksaitis, M. K. F. (2016). *Servant leaders' use of high-performance work practices and corporate social performance* (Doctoral dissertation). (Order No. 10182916). Available from ProQuest Dissertations & Theses Global: The Humanities and Social Sciences Collection. (1835080950). Retrieved from https://search-proquest-com.libraryresources.columbiasouthern.edu/docview/1835080950?a

ccountid=33337

Riordan, C. M. (2010, March 3). Nice guys may finish last at work.

Retrieved from http://articles.cnn.com/2010-03-

03/living/cb.nice.guys.finish.last_1_nicetrait-successful-

manager?_s=PM:LIVING.

Robinson, H. W. (2015). Two traits of agape love. *Journal of the*

Evangelical Homiletics Society, 15(2), 60–63.

Ross-Grant, L. (2016). *Exploring the relationships between*

leadership styles and job satisfaction among employees of nonprofit

organizations (Doctoral dissertation or master's thesis). (Order No.

10111462). Available from ProQuest Dissertations & Theses Global:

The Humanities and Social Sciences Collection. Retrieved from

https://libraryresources.columbiasouthern.edu/login?url=http://searc

h.proquest.com.libraryresources.columbiasouthern.edu/docview/179

8478720?accountid=33337. (1798478720)

Seale, C. (1999). Quality in qualitative research. *Qualitative Inquiry,*

5(4), 465–478.

See-Kwong, G., & Zhen-Jie, B. L. (2013). The influence of servant

leadership towards organizational commitment: The mediating role of trust in leaders. *International Journal of Business and Management*, 9(1), 17–25. Retrieved from http://www.ccsenet.org/ijbm

Self, C. L. S. (2009). *Love and organizational leadership: An intertexture analysis of 1 Corinthians 13* (Doctoral dissertation or master's thesis). (Order No. 3377775). Available from ProQuest Dissertations & Theses Global: The Humanities and Social Sciences Collection. Retrieved from https://search-proquest-com.libraryresources.columbiasouthern.edu/docview/305136202?accountid=33337. (305136202)

Sendjaya, S., Sarros, J., & Santora, J. (2008). Defining and measuring servant leadership behavior in organizations. *Journal of Management Studies*, 45, 402–424.

Sokoll S. (2014) Servant leadership and employee commitment to a supervisor. *International Journal of Leadership Studies*, 8(2). Retrieved from http://www.regent.edu/acad/global/publications/ijls/new/vol8iss2/5-Sokoll.pdf.

Smith, S. (2006). Encouraging the use of reflexivity in the writing up of qualitative research. *International Journal of Therapeutic Rehabilitation, 13*: 209–214.

Spears, L. C. (2010). Character and servant leadership: Ten characteristics of effective, caring leaders. *The Journal of Virtues & Leadership, 1*(1), 25–30.

Spears, L. C., ed. (1995). *Reflections on leadership: How Robert K. Greenleaf's theory of servant-leadership influenced today's top management thinkers.* New York, NY: John Wiley & Sons.

Spears, L. C. (2005). The understanding and practice of servant-leadership. *Servant Leadership Research Roundtable.* Retrieved from http://www.regent.edu/acad/sls/publications/conference_proceedings /servant_leadership_roundtable/2005/pdf/spears_practice.pdf.

Sprecher, S., & Fehr, B. (2005). Compassionate love for close others and humanity. *Journal of Social and Personal Relationships, 22,* 629–651. Doi or journal's home page url?

Sullivan, S. A. (2017). *Leadership amore: Love as the art and science of leadership* (Order No. 10663167). Available from ProQuest Dissertations & Theses Global: The Humanities and Social

Sciences Collection. (1941682023). Retrieved from https://search-proquest-com.libraryresources.columbiasouthern.edu/docview/1941682023?accountid=33337.

Swenson, C. H., Nelson, M. K., Warner, J., & Dunlap, D. (1992). Scale of Feelings and Behavior of Love: revised. In L. Vandeereek, S. Knapp, & T. L. Jackson (Eds.), *Innovations in clinical practice: A source book* (Vol. 11, pp. 303–314). Sarasota, FL. Professional Resource Press.

Takaaki, H. (2014). Philia as agapē: The theme of friendship in the gospel of John. *Asia Journal of Theology, 28,* 250–262.

Tanno, J. (2017). *Servant leadership: What makes it an effective leadership model* (Doctoral dissertation or master's thesis). (Order No. 10604029). Available from ProQuest Dissertations & Theses Global: The Humanities and Social Sciences Collection. Retrieved from https://search-proquest-com.libraryresources.columbiasouthern.edu/docview/1936708382?accountid=33337. (1936708382)

Van Dierendonck, D., & Nuijten, I. (2011). The servant leadership survey: Development and validation of a multidimensional measure. *Journal of Business and Psychology, 26*(3), 249–267.

Wilson, D. F. (2013). *Servant Leadership and Job Satisfaction in a Multicultural Hospitality Organization: A Quantitative, Non-experimental Descriptive Study*. Grand Canyon University. Retrieved from http://pqdtopen.proquest.com/pubnum/3597448.html

Zentner, Aeron. (2015). *Servant Leadership and Religious Values: Drawing Speculation to Commonalities between Servant Leadership Characteristics and Faith-Based Values*. Leadership & Organizational Behavior. 10.2139/ssrn.2638587.

Appendix A

Consent Form

Contact: Researcher

Dustin Hofheins, MBA

(801) 814-3615

dustinhofheins@gmail.com

Servant Leadership: A Better Way to do Business.

You are being asked to take part in a research study that will explore the role of love in servant leadership. Please read this form carefully and ask any questions you may have before agreeing to take part in the study.

What the study is about: The purpose of this study is to examine how servant leaders view love and leadership. You must consider yourself a servant leader and have five years of leadership experience.

What we will ask you to do: If you agree to be in this study, we will conduct an interview with you. The interview will include questions regarding the role of love in servant leadership. The interview will take about 30 minutes to complete. With your permission, we would also like to tape-record the interview.

Risks and benefits: I do not anticipate any risks to you participating in this study other than those encountered in day-to-day life. There are no benefits to you.

Compensation: There is not compensation. A copy of the research findings will be provided to all participants at their request.

Your answers will be confidential. The records of this study will be kept private. In any sort of report, we make public we will not include any information that will make it possible to identify you. Research records will be kept in a locked file; only the researcher will have access to the records. If we tape-record the interview, we will destroy the tape after it has been transcribed, which we anticipate will be within two months of its taping. Transcription is required to be held for three years, will be held in a safe, will only be accessible by the researcher, and will be destroyed after the holding time.

Taking part is voluntary: Taking part in this study is completely voluntary. You may skip any questions that you do not want to answer. If you decide not to take part or to skip some of the questions, it will not affect your current or future relationship. If you decide to take part, you are free to withdraw at any time.

If you have questions: The researcher conducting this study is Dustin Hofheins. Please ask any questions you have now. If you have questions later, you may contact Dustin Hofheins at dustinhofheins@gmail.com.

Statement of Consent: I have read the above information and have received answers to any questions I asked. I consent to take part in the study.

Your Signature _____ Date

_____

Your Name (printed)

_____

_____

In addition to agreeing to participate, I also consent to having the interview tape-recorded.

Your Signature _____ Date

_____

Signature of person obtaining consent

_____ Date _____

Printed name of person obtaining consent

_____ Date _____

This consent form will be kept by the researcher for at least three

years beyond the end of the study.

Appendix B

Interview Guide

Participant Alias:

Position(s):

Gender: M or F

1. This study defines love as, not a romantic love, but as an action verb meaning that when we love others, we serve them. In what ways do you see yourself as a leader who possesses love for others?

2. This study defines servant leadership as a leadership theory that asserts that leadership is about serving those in whom the leader has stewardship over. What role does love play in servant leadership?

3. Is there anything that prevents you from utilizing love as a servant leader? If so, what?

4. What do you think is the significance of love in today's leadership culture?

5. Have you found yourself in a particular situation where a leader was needed who possessed great love for others? If so, could you please explain the situation and how it was handled?

6. What additional thoughts would you like to share regarding the role that love plays in servant leadership?